R.I.S.E., BLACK CHILD

By Dr. Darlene Powell-Garlington
© 2005 Dr. Darlene Powell-Garlington

All rights reserved. No part of this book may be reproduced or utilized in any form or by any means, electronic or mechanical, including photocopying, recording, or by any information storage or retrieval system, without permission in writing from the publisher.

Inquiries should be addressed to Dr. Darlene Retreat Center, PO Box 597, Marion, CT 06444.

ISBN: 0-9766378-0-4
© 2005 by Dr. Darlene Powell-Garlington

R.I.S.E., BLACK CHILD:
Developing Racial Identity and Self-Esteem
in African American Children

Acknowledgments

My husband, Dr. Ernest C. Garlington, is my rock. He has taught me to rely on God for divine guidance in parenting skills. The protection and provision he gives our family allow us to pursue our individual dreams and bring them to fruition. Ernie's belief in my work inspired me to assume greater creative and literary control of this project and decide to self-publish.

God's grace and blessings have guided me in raising two wonderful children, who teach me more about love and my divine purpose every day. Dotti is 17 and a freshman at a Historically Black University. Derek is 12 and an honor student, now attending 8th grade at a predominately White, independent school. I thank you both for putting up with Mommy's passions, supporting my work and contributing to the process.

My parents, Robert and Leanna Powell, have given me more love, guidance and support than any daughter could dream of having. Without them, I would not be who I am or have developed positive self-esteem and racial identity. My accomplishments and achievements are theirs, too. This work is a family legacy.

The title, *R.I.S.E., Black Child*, is the creative brainpower of my big brother and only sibling, Robert L. Powell, Jr. His work in the Boys and Girls Club, as a high school counselor, and as a basketball coach motivates and inspires me in my work with children and youth.

TABLE OF CONTENTS

Introduction 7
   Effects of Racial Identity and Self-Esteem on
     Academic Achievement 7
   What a Difference Two Decades Make 10
   The Difference Is You. 12

Chapter One: Building Blocks – Racial Identity 16
   Racial Identity: Membership Has its Privileges 16
   Stages of Racial Identity 19
   Racial Identity Assessment Tool.................. 20
   Racial Identity Builders 21

Chapter Two: Building Blocks – Self-Image
and Self-Esteem 24
   Self-Image: The Child in the Mirror................ 25
   Self-Esteem: The Power of the Mind 26
   Self-Esteem Assessment Tool..................... 27
   Self-Esteem Builders 28

Chapter Three: Building Blocks – Racial Identity,
Self-Esteem, and Academic Achievement 31
   Racial Identity and Self-Esteem: A Winning
     Combination 33
   Racial Identity and Self-Esteem Assessment Tool....... 34
   Racial Identity and Self-Esteem at Every Level 36
   R.I.S.E., Black Child 37

Chapter Four: Infants and Babies 40
   Spare the Rod 41
   Reactions to Strangers 42
   Achievement for Babies........................ 42

Chapter Five: Toddlers—Ages 18 Months to 36 Months 48
- Safety Measures.................................. 49
- Learn by Example 49
- Daycare Beware!.................................. 50
- Cues from Child's Play........................... 51
- Make Your "Net Work" 52
- Milestones to Watch.............................. 52
- Achievement for Toddlers 53

Chapter Six: Preschool and Kindergarten—Ages Three to Six Years................................ 56
- Images: Near and Far............................. 56
- Language: Watching Your Words 58
- Milestones to Watch.............................. 59
- Achievement for Preschoolers and Kindergarteners 59

Chapter Seven: School-Age Children 65
- Teachers: The Role They Play 66
- Standardized Testing 68
- Black Boys and the School System 69
- White Schools versus Black Schools 71
- Milestones for School-Age Children 73
- Achievement for School-Age Children.............. 74

Chapter Eight: Adolescence—Thirteen Years of Age and Older 78
- Positively (or Negatively) Black................. 80
- No Time for Kidding 81
- Peer Relations 82
- Milestones for Adolescents....................... 82
- Academic Achievement for Adolescents............. 83

Chapter Nine: The Role of Family 88
Strengths of the Black Family 88
Family Assessment Tool 90

Chapter Ten: The Role of School 93
Teachers Can Make a Difference 94
Getting Passing Grades for Our Schools 95
School Assessment Tool 96

Chapter Eleven: The Role of the Community 99
Community Assessment Tool 100

Chapter Twelve: God Is in Charge! 103
God's In Charge 105

APPENDIX 107
Sentence Completion 108
Parent Questionnaire 110
Afrocentric Interventions for Psychologists, Social
   Workers, and Mental Health Professionals 113
In-Home Interventions 115
Clinical Diagnosis and Goals 115
Nguzo Saba 118

Resources 133
Education 133
For Parents 133
Recreational 134

ABOUT THE AUTHOR 135

Introduction

Effects of Racial Identity and Self-Esteem on Academic Achievement

It's not uncommon for Black children to show evidence of self-image and self-esteem challenges. That's why parents, teachers and caregivers need to be aware of the signs, assess the situation, and intervene effectively. You may wonder what you need to look for in a child that has problems with their self-image and self-esteem. Here are some signs:

- Children who visibly look as if they are frustrated or if they are feeling anxious. Black children are strong users of nonverbal communication and their feelings are often visible. Body language, such as looking down, slumping in the seat or fidgeting a great deal is a key indicator of such emotions.
- Children who fail to finish their assignments. These children might have a fear of failure ("I won't get a good grade anyway, so why try?"), fear of success, or just lack of motivation altogether. Whatever the case, they avoid putting forth their full effort toward schoolwork because they don't think they can handle the results.
- Children who are disruptive, hostile, or defiant. This protective mechanism may be fear resulting from some perceived hurt, such as mistreatment in a previous academic environment. Teachers who have negative expectations of these children make matters worse.
- Children who constantly make excuses for their poor performance. Their excuses are an attempt to maintain some sense of dignity but they have such negative impressions of themselves, they are afraid to try.

- Children who have a poor attention span or daydream. They may lack motivation to participate and may not have the confidence to succeed. They also fail to see how the subject matter is relevant to their daily lives.
- Children who have poor eye contact. In some families, direct eye contact is a sign of disrespect, particularly if the child is communicating with an adult or White person. Other Black children might avoid someone's eyes because they think that the person dislikes them. Black youth, who may be particularly proficient in nonverbal communication, can detect this type of bias toward them.
- Children who won't even try a new task. This is a sign that they fear failure and believe that best way to avoid failing is not to make an attempt. They lack self-confidence.
- Children who dislike the teacher, school, or both. These children are potential dropouts. Interestingly enough, their response may have to do with the message they're receiving from the teacher. Studies indicate that students who perceive their teachers as unhappy with their jobs or as biased toward them, dislike school.
- Children who don't participate in class. They lack motivation from the teacher and think that their answers or behavior will be misunderstood or ridiculed. Other Black students in this category are responding to their teacher's perception of them. If the teacher doesn't want them to volunteer, they won't. The way the teacher perceives them becomes a self-fulfilling prophecy.
- Children who are constantly late or absent. Skipping class or cutting school is a way for them to avoid uncomfortable situations. If they really don't want to be

in school (or class), they'll find it hard to get there on time.
- Children who don't involve themselves with other students. They are afraid to interact with others because they feel threatened or are uncomfortable in the environment. Differences in culture, class or race may contribute to the child's feelings of isolation.

It's no secret that Black parents are still dealing with issues of racism when it comes to raising Black children. Although it's been fifteen years since I wrote my book, *Different and Wonderful: Raising Black Children in a Race-Conscious Society*, a work based on my dissertation research, I still witness the problems that result from racial identity and self-esteem issues that exist in Black children. These factors affect our children's development in various areas of their lives. The issues of racial identity and self-esteem are particularly relevant when we look at low achievement scores and academic performance. Children who don't know how to cope with the race consciousness and occasional overt racism that continues to pervade American society are typically frustrated in school environments. In addition, children who don't have a positive view of Black people and a sense of self-efficacy are not likely to excel in school. I have faced challenges in educating my own two children. These experiences, as well as my advocacy for the families with whom I work, have given me additional approaches to help our children. A wide achievement gap exists in our school system today. Our children are failing, but we have yet to look at how we are failing them. Until we take responsibility for our part of the problem, we will never realize the solution. I believe the information bound in the pages of *R.I.S.E, Black Child* will provide you with some basic instruction on how you can help your children change their perceptions about how they view themselves and their abilities. This is the first step toward making a difference in the classroom.

What a Difference Two Decades Make

It's been twenty years since I replicated the famous study conducted in the late 1930s by Drs. Kenneth and Mamie Clark. This was the premise for my first book. In that classic study, researchers found that 67 percent of Black children preferred to play with a White doll instead of a Black doll. This research was used in the landmark decision of *Brown vs. the Board of Education*, illustrating that an educational system that is separate could never be equal because Black children still associate "Whiteness" with being better or superior. In addition, the resources and equipment in the White schools were far more plentiful and updated. In my 1985 study, years after the Civil Rights movement, the results had barely changed. Forty years later, 65 percent of the Black children surveyed chose White dolls over Black ones. The message was the same as before: "We're not as good, as pretty, or as nice as Whites. We don't like being Black. We wish we could be like them."

My research took things a step further. Once I identified that the problem still existed, I looked for solutions. I designed an intervention to encourage the children to take a positive view of Blackness and to select Black dolls. After the children made their selections, my researchers and I made our own doll choices. We told our young participants that we preferred the Black dolls. We then used positive adjectives when we referred to the Black dolls and read stories depicting Black children in positive ways. When we performed the test again, 68 percent of the Black children in the study picked the Black dolls. In only a few minutes, we proved that positive modeling and reinforcement can have a great impact on Black children's racial identity and self-esteem.

Although the solutions are not that easy, the goal is to use these approaches to help children internalize and maintain positive racial identity and self-esteem. Pro-Black does not mean anti-White. Our children are able to accept others from different races and to embrace diversity when they first love themselves. Of course, having access to Black role models is critical. However, White teachers can also have a tremendous impact on the Black children in their classroom. If a teacher is encouraging, culturally proficient, and supports Black children in experiencing academic success, the race of the teacher does not matter.

I recommended that parents, teachers, mental health professionals, and concerned family members do the same things that were done in the research so that they could develop strong, confident, high-achieving, self-assured Black children.

I'm pleased to report that there has been a lot of progress since then. When the research was conducted in 1985, there were very few Black dolls on the market. Those Black dolls that were on the market were merely White dolls painted Black. Since then, I've consulted with Mattel and Tyco Toys to develop more realistic Black dolls. In addition, there have been a plethora of Black people who have opened their own companies to develop Black dolls. As a result, the whole market, in terms of Black dolls, has changed and Black children have more choices.

Due to all of the media focus on racial diversity and sensitivity, people have become more sensitive to issues surrounding racial identity and self-esteem in Black children. To some degree, there has been more acknowledgment of the contributions made by Black people and some of that information has been integrated in the classrooms. Multiculturalism and cultural competence are viewed as necessary for a progressive school system. However, there is still more to do, especially in the area of academic achievement. Despite attempts to help Black children feel better about themselves, these attempts do little to help our children compete on the educational front. According to the

National Assessment of Educational Progress, the official report card on how America's children are doing in our schools, 63 percent of Black fourth graders had "below basic" reading skills in 2000, and that gap continues to widen. The situation gets worse as children get older; they fall further behind as they reach higher grade levels.

When looking at the achievement gap, it is important to note that socio-economic status is more a factor than race. Poor White children also score low on achievement tests. Unfortunately, there is a large percentage of Black children living in poverty. These children are just as capable when given exposure to prerequisite skills and educational resources. This suggests that it's imperative that every parent, grandparent, relative, foster parent/guardian and anyone else responsible for raising children, acts now to ensure that these children have everything they need for educational success. I believe that racial identity and self-esteem are essential components for academic excellence.

The Difference Is You

Boosting self-esteem and developing positive racial identity in Black children requires much more than just putting a few pictures on the wall or talking about Black leaders every February, especially if we're talking specifically about academic achievement. As parents, we need to develop an ongoing, integrative process to convince our youth that not only is academic success expected of them, it's a divine right that has been passed along to them from our Creator and our ancestors. Black children need to not only know that they have the capacity to do well in school, but that they need to be provided with clear examples of other successful African Americans who excel on all fronts.

For White children, having White examples of success is the

norm. The lesson plans in schools have traditionally favored them. The stories and legacies of Leif Erickson, Alexander Graham Bell, and Abraham Lincoln are revered and repeated throughout all grade levels. The White student can see the lineage and inherently feel a connection to this country. Eurocentric textbooks reinforce White superiority at the exclusion of the vast contributions of non-Whites to America. The experiences of a Black child converge with the discovery that in all likelihood, their ancestor's American experience began in chains. The stigma of slavery dovetails with terms such as "minority," "underprivileged," and "at-risk." These phrases belittle Black students and kill their enthusiasm for learning. It's no wonder that Black students, like the youngsters in our study, come to believe that "Whiteness" is better than "Blackness." This belief has a great impact on their overall behavior and performance.

As we examine the information we communicate to our students, we should also assess what information is excluded. The countless contributions of African Americans across the panorama of science, culture and the arts are marginalized, if mentioned at all. Thus, Black students have the added burden of sitting in classrooms that promote White intellectual superiority as a fact, by virtue of the information that the teachers highlight on a daily basis. This challenge affects African Americans across all socio-economic levels. Black celebrities from all over the country have contacted me to ask how they can help their children deal with racial identity and self-esteem issues, despite their access to exclusive educational systems. I recently appeared on *Good Morning America* with Diane Sawyer, to discuss an interview with comedian Chris Rock, where he disclosed his concerns about how racism hurts Black boys and his fear of raising a son. Chris noted that he was glad that he was raising a daughter, and no matter how much money you have, there are times when your child will be called the N-word. At the same time, Blacks in impoverished communities also seek advice on dealing with these problems.

I say the solution starts with you. Black children need to R.I.S.E. Being able to R.I.S.E involves developing strong Racial (R) Identity (I) and Self- (S) Esteem (E). Black children with these positive characteristics get higher grades in school and do better in life. This guide will provide you with the tools, strategies and techniques to empower yourself and empower and motivate your children. With specific examples, this guide will demonstrate how what you say and do can have a great impact on how your child perceives himself and the world around him, as well as how these perceptions impact his academic achievement. Once you complete this guide, that's only a first step toward a resolution. It's up to you to put what you've learned into practice so that your child can effectively integrate into society as well as compete and excel academically. Most importantly, incorporating the elements of racial identity and self-esteem for academic excellence will ensure that your child takes her rightful place among our high-achieving ancestors.

Chapter One: Building Blocks – Racial Identity

Are you a card-carrying member of the African American race? Some Blacks say yes, others don't know, and the remaining folks don't really care. You should care because children excel in environments that affirm and celebrate them. As a parent, if you start this process in your home, your children will begin to internalize these values.

In this chapter, we discuss what it means to be African American, assess whether your children have issues with racial identity, and offer strategies for helping children make improvements.

Racial Identity: Membership Has its Privileges

Seven-year-old Jasmine was sent to the principal's office for cutting her classmate's hair with a pair of scissors. Jasmine told her parents that she was just playing hairdresser and didn't mean to hurt her friend, Suzie. The girls have been socializing since preschool. During their times together, Suzie would frequently take her long hair out of her ponytail and fling it behind her back. Sometimes, Jasmine tried to imitate Suzie but since her hair was in cornrows it didn't move. Then Jasmine would try to braid Suzie's hair, but it would escape the braid and pull free.

Every day Jasmine's mother would braid Jasmine's hair for school. Jasmine would say, "Mommy, please let me wear my hair like Suzie's." Her mom would shake her head. "You can't wear your hair out because it will puff up and look uncombed," she warned. "When you get older, I'll put a relaxer in your hair so you can look pretty like Suzie." That comment alone was enough to keep Jasmine content until the next morning.

If we look at the example above, Jasmine's mother didn't realize that she was saying anything to negatively impact her daughter's racial identity. Jasmine's mom sought a quick solution and responded in a manner that she thought would appease her daughter. What Jasmine's mom thought was a quick fix was really a slow leak. Each time Jasmine was told that a hair relaxer was the solution to her hair "problems," any positive things she believed about herself and her Blackness seeped away. The message Jasmine heard was, "YOU ARE NOT PRETTY NOW. YOU ARE NOT AS PRETTY AS SUZIE. SUZIE IS WHITE. YOU ARE BLACK. SHE IS PRETTY. YOU ARE NOT."

Racial identity, where each of us determines the personal significance and social meaning of belonging to a particular racial group, can have a significant impact on your child's success. If your child has received messages about Black people that have been negative, then his behavior could be the result of that self-fulfilling prophecy. Alternatively, exposure to positive images will help shape your child's positive racial identity. Beyond that, your racial identity not only affects how you behave, but can also impact how others interact with you.

In an interview on National Public Radio, Beverly Daniel Tatum, president of Spelman College, a historically Black women's school, and the author of *Why Are All the Black Kids Sitting Together in the Cafeteria?*, specifically addressed this point. "When you are growing up, whether as a young African American or Latino or Asian or Native American or a White person, your racial membership plays a role in how people perceive you, respond to you. So it is, of course, a part of your identity, just as your gender is a part of your identity or your ethnic background or religious tradition because it shapes how you have experienced the world and how people in the world experience you."

In the case of little Jasmine, her friend Suzie might have unknowingly reinforced Jasmine's negative views about herself. The more impressed Jasmine was with Suzie's hair, the more Suzie was motivated to flaunt it. Effective parent intervention is key here. Instead of telling her daughter to wait for a hair relaxer, Jasmine's mother should have focused on trying to make her daughter proud of her own hair by insisting that Jasmine's hair was just as beautiful as her classmate's hair. When doing this, it's important that Jasmine's mother not encourage her daughter to see her friend's hair type as something negative. There are ranges of beauty and children can be proud of themselves as well as appreciate the beauty of others.

In fact, individuals who have positive racial identity are more likely to build healthy relationships with people from varied backgrounds. Despite what critics say, people with racial identity do not widen the gap between the races. In addition, promoting racial identity in your child is not the same as encouraging your child to be racist. Pro-Black is not anti-White. Ideally, we'd like to live in a society where race does not matter. Where, as Martin Luther King described, people are judged by the content of their character and not the color of their skin. Even if such a world existed, people would still exhibit differences within the "human race," and that's a good thing. As Tatum points out in her NPR interview, "There are still going to be differences in terms of cultural expression. There are going to be differences in terms of religious beliefs and assumptions. There are going to be differences in experience as a result of geographic affiliation or gender. There are going to be differences that are important and rich, much like the analogy of the salad bowl. You know you want a variety of flavors in that salad bowl, and to bring those things together you don't want to necessarily puree them all into a tasteless mess." When you appreciate the differences in yourself, you can appreciate the flavors others bring to the mix.

Stages of Racial Identity

William Cross, Jr. outlined a five-stage model of how Black Americans develop racial identity. In stage one, *the pre-encounter stage*, a Black person believes in White superiority. In stage two, *the encounter stage*, a Black person adopts a pro-Black, anti-White philosophy. There is an intense search for Black identity. In the third stage, *immersion-emersion*, the person has an overwhelming desire to understand the Black experience, African American history and the Black community. Stage four is *internalization,* where the person becomes disillusioned and returns back to stage one. In stage five, *internalization commitment*, the person develops a sense of connectedness with all oppressed people. She has a genuine concern for anyone disadvantaged or mistreated. Self-esteem and racial identity are high.

Cross believes, and I concur, that this is a necessary step in Black Americans' individual development. By combining our outrage at racism with our Black pride and self-esteem, we can formulate action that promotes our full participation in American society. Such action can begin when we recognize the Black community for what it is: an effective support system with traditions worth preserving. It also requires that we value our own unique talents and abilities.

Differences and uniqueness are a huge benefit as long as you don't use those differences to discriminate or isolate. That's why children with a strong racial identity are essential to the communities where they live. By learning about themselves, they have gifts that can be shared with other people. Think of the last time you enjoyed a multicultural event at your church or job: I'm sure you enjoyed tasting the various foods, seeing different dances, and learning interesting facts about another community. Your children will also enjoy such an exchange and, through racial identity, they'll have a lot more to offer. It's only when parents make a point of generalizing and labeling "White people" as bad or evil, do they run the risk of corrupting their children's minds and tainting their point of view. This type of "negativity" really isn't about racial identity; it's about a parent being so irresponsible that he projects his negative views onto his children without thinking about the consequences. You *can* inspire self-pride without perpetuating external hatred and parents need to know that loving yourself and loving others are not mutually exclusive. To be a complete individual, you need to do both.

Racial Identity Assessment Tool

How would you know if your child has issues with racial identity? As with anything else, listen to the source. Although your child may not use the exact words to indicate trouble in this area, there are some things that you can look for to make conclusions on your own. Review the following statements to see if they apply to your child, then read the explanation below for further guidance:

- Prefers White dolls/action figures
- Prefers light skin or White people
- Expresses hate or negativity toward all White people
- Sees Black people as less intelligent
- Dislikes or isn't interested in Black history
- Dislikes their features (hair, lips, nose, skin color)
- Rejects music by Black artists
- Is embarrassed around relatives who speak Ebonics
- Is more comfortable in White social environments
- Is only comfortable in Black social environments

The above indicators represent key areas that need to be assessed when determining your child's sense of racial identity. Part of your responsibility, as a mother or father, is to determine whether your child does have problems with racial identity, and then do whatever you can to resolve those issues.

As you review these, you may notice that you also have issues related to one or more of these areas. As you help your child develop his racial identity, it's important that you also resolve these areas in your life.

Racial Identity Builders

African Americans who have internalized the commonplace understandings of race that are based on stereotypes and inaccuracies, are less likely to want to be affiliated with that race and may tend to de-emphasize that aspect of themselves. For example, if you think of Black people only in terms of slavery, how they measure up to other races on the economic scale, or view Black people as being "less than" White people, then you certainly wouldn't want to identify yourself as a member of the Black race. That's why some African Americans we know, who are obviously Black, deny their race—they've internalized the negative things society says about Black people and haven't developed any arguments to provide a more balanced view. As parents, it's our job to put the things that our children see in perspective and provide a more balanced viewpoint whenever possible. In that way, our children can begin to embrace all aspects of their Blackness.

If you're ready to help your child develop a strong sense of racial identity, here are some things you can do:
- **Talk to your children about race.** It's important that you tell your children what you want them to know about race. Don't just rely on their teachers or other students. You should provide your child with your understanding of how Black people fit into society and what that means for our future.
- **Talk to your children about slavery.** It's important that you provide your own explanation about slavery so you can field any questions your child has and put the

experience in the proper perspective. Let your child know that the chains of the past do not keep Black people in bondage.

- **Provide supplemental educational materials for your child.** Whether your child goes to a predominately White or predominately Black school, it's important that you have books, videos, magazines, and other materials in your home that represent Black people in a positive light. This sends a message to your child about your views and you can ensure that your child is getting the right information.
- **Encourage diverse friendships.** Again, racial identity is not about loving yourself at the exclusion of others. It's about loving yourself and appreciating the differences in other people. Encourage your children to develop friendships with people of various races, so they will develop confidence in dealing with diverse groups of people over the long term.
- **Be honest.** As we share information with our children, we must tell the whole truth. There are areas in the Black community that need to be addressed. While we should never dwell on our shortcomings, its important that you discuss these issues so your children understand what the issues are. This helps them to have a balanced perspective and distinguish the truth from a lie when they come across it.
- **Put God first.** Let your children know that regardless of what information they learn about race, it will never replace the information they know about God. They need to identify themselves as children of God first, knowing that God made them for His divine purpose and their race and nationality are not accidents, but more of God's precious gifts.

Chapter Two: Building Blocks – Self-Image and Self-Esteem

Children's minds are just like sponges. They soak up everything we say and do. That's why it's extremely important that we choose our words very carefully and ensure that we closely monitor our behavior as well. What we do for our children today can have a great impact on their future development. As parents, we provide the building blocks that help shape their views about themselves and the world.

You might ask, how can you prevent yourself from harming your child, if you don't even know you're doing it? The answer isn't a simple one. At the very least, err on the side of caution. Be very aware of how you're communicating with your child. Avoid saying negative statements about your child's hair, complexion, weight, height or intellectual ability. Read as much as you can with regard to child development and ask lots of questions. Most importantly, once you know better, do better. Many of us do know that some of things that we say to our children are not constructive, but we say them anyway. Stop! Take this opportunity to reaffirm your commitment as a parent—a good parent. Then search for specific ways that you can help your child's development.

In this chapter, we'll focus on the building blocks—self-image and self-esteem—because our success in these areas is essential if we truly want to raise healthy, self-confident African American children. More specifically, we'll define these terms, look at why they're so important, and offer specific strategies for helping our children excel in these areas.

Self-Image: The Child in the Mirror

Tommy was really excited about trying out for the football team. Unfortunately, when he hit the field, he felt really uncomfortable around the other players. Tommy was just about five feet six inches tall, while the other guys were well over six feet. Additionally, Tommy was 140 pounds while his competition weighed in at least 200 pounds each. "Show us what you got, little man," the coach joked. Tommy looked at the coach, then back at the other players. Instead of taking his spot on the field, he picked up his belongings and raced down the street until he got to the front door of his house.

"What happened at practice?" his father breathlessly asked when Tommy entered the room. As soon as the last word left his lips, he could sense that tryouts hadn't gone very well. "You'll get 'em next time," he encouraged. Despite Tommy's half-hearted smile, the fourteen-year-old knew that he'd never measure up to the guys that were on the field and he'd already concluded that there wouldn't be a next time.

When your child looks in the mirror, who does he see looking back at him? The answer to that question has to do with self-image, which describes how we see ourselves compared to other people. Self-image includes what we believe we look like physically; how our personality comes across; what kind of people we think we are; and what kind of people others think we are. As described in the example above, a negative self-image can prevent us from attempting to succeed at the things we really want. Tommy declared defeat before he tried out for the team. Similarly, your child's negative self-image could hinder your child's success at extracurricular activities and academic performance.

As a parent, you are one of the first people to interact with your child, so you have a big responsibility when it comes to helping your child develop a positive self-image. Initially, our perceptions about ourselves are based on the scripts we have been given from the first people who interacted with us. As we grow, our self-image is influenced by how we assess various factors in our lives, such as friendships; church; peer groups; family relationships; academic achievements; athletic abilities; and physical appearance, as well as the roles we play in our various environments (e.g. home, school, work and the community). At some point you'll notice your child comparing himself to the other children in his environment, in an effort to learn about the world around him. Your son might develop a fascination with eyes after noticing that his are brown. Your daughter might be interested in other people's hair after discovering her own thick, curly hair. It's after drawing conclusions about these aspects that we develop labels for ourselves, as well as our own scripts for how we think we should behave, according to our self-image.

Perhaps the first lesson we should teach our children about self-image is that we are wonderfully made in the image of God. If you consistently talk about the beauty of your son's tightly curled hair, he'll also think his hair is beautiful. At the same time, if you're constantly complaining about his "nappy" hair, then he'll come to resent his hair and find it inferior when he compares it to other types of hair. The same occurs when you refer to your child's other characteristics, like complexion, weight and height. Whatever you emphasize consistently, will become important to your child. Whatever you praise will be praised by your child, too. This is how we can help our children form healthy mental pictures of themselves.

Self-Esteem: The Power of the Mind

Why is having a positive self-image important? Your child's self-image influences your child's self-esteem, which is the way your child perceives his self-worth and the feelings that he has about his self-image. If your child feels negatively about himself, he has low self-esteem. Similarly, if he feels positively about himself, he is said to have high self-esteem. No one loves everything about himself or herself at all times. What you need to know is how your child views himself *most* of the time.

Fortunately, positive self-esteem can be taught. It's not a magical gene that has to be inside you when you're born. You can ensure that your children have high self-esteem, which will enable them to have the courage to take risks; develop their abilities, skills, and talents; and establish healthy friendships. As children of God, we see ourselves as capable and equal to others. Teach children that they are valuable due to God's grace. Self-esteem is not arrogance, being haughty, or looking down on others. In fact, people who relate this way usually have low self-esteem. As a first step in helping your child improve his self-esteem, you should take time to determine what issues may or may not exist.

Self-Esteem Assessment Tool

Are you wondering if your child has any self-esteem issues? Read the following statements and see if any of them apply to your child:
- Doesn't feel liked by peers
- Self-conscious or easily embarrassed
- Seems unresponsive to attention and praise
- Too shy, timid, fearful or anxious
- Wants excessive attention
- Stubborn, sullen or irritable
- Often lonely and isolated
- Says negative self statements and self-deprecating remarks
- Doesn't like his appearance
- Complains about not being able to do things

Each of the choices above is a sign of low self-esteem. As a parent, you need to constantly connect with your child to see if he is experiencing any of these feelings. If so, it's up to you to start putting some strategies into play to help your child feel good and if you can't do it, don't be afraid to turn to someone who can (seek help from your pastor or school counselor, for example). Don't stop there. Look for ways to boost your child's confidence on daily basis.

Don't be surprised if, as you start to build your child's self-esteem, you start to feel good as well. As you find joy in your children's triumphs, you'll also want to tackle some goals of your own, so that you can find joy in your own accomplishments. Additionally, the more adept you become at helping your child develop confidence, the more confident you'll become in your own parenting skills. Good self-esteem will start to rub off on you.

Self-Esteem Builders

The good news is that you have the power to build positive self-esteem in your children. Here are a few suggestions to help you get started:

- **Shower your youngster with praise and appreciation.** Be sincere in the way you express your appreciation, because children can spot a phony. Commit to being generous with your love and always respect your children by saying "please" and "thank you." Those practices will go a long way in letting your children know they are important and that they have value.
- **Cheer them on.** You should be your child's biggest cheerleader. The encouragement will boost his esteem and self-worth. Also, encourage your youngster to make his own decisions. This will help him feel more confident when finalizing choices.
- **Speak highly of them.** Toot your child's horn. If she's done something good, talk about it and make sure she

hears you. If you're proud, show it. Thank God for His blessings and let your child know that she is doing something that is pleasing God. This positive reinforcement will inspire them to find other ways to get encouraging feedback, and that will ultimately increase her self-esteem.

- **Practice the Golden Rule.** Treat your child as you'd want to be treated. I know some people don't feel that way when it comes to anyone under 18, but children want and deserve to be treated with respect, kindness, and consideration. Every time you patronize your child, belittle him, and put him down, you're chipping away at his confidence. Instead of breaking him down, build him up.
- **Help them deal with failure.** Part of your responsibility as a parent is helping your child keep things in perspective, convincing him to triumph over tragedies, and motivating him to persevere in the midst of perceived impossibilities. You should be his mentor and shining example.

What messages are you sending your children? What things are you doing to shape their views about themselves and the world? If they're not things to help build your youngster's self-esteem, then you need to make a drastic change. If you're already doing some of things mentioned here, then find some additional tools to implement. You can never do too much when it comes to making your child feel good about himself.

Chapter Three: Building Blocks – Racial Identity, Self-Esteem, and Academic Achievement

Andre was an honor student until he reached the ninth grade. Even though the schoolwork was no problem for him, Andre became distracted by his classmates. The teasing he received from his peers was starting to take a toll. Every time Andre would raise his hand with the right answer, someone would crack a joke or yell out a wisecrack. During breaks, the Black kids in the class constantly referred to Andre as "the nerd." A few times, some of them accused him of "acting White" because of the way he spoke. Andre became confused. When he told his parents about the teasing, they simply told him to ignore it. That wasn't easy for Andre because he desperately wanted to fit in. It seemed as long as he got good grades, he would never truly be "down" with the cool kids in the school.

One day, Andre found a solution. He stopped going to Honor Society meetings and refused to do his homework. When the teacher asked for a volunteer, Andre would call out funny answers to make the class laugh. This irritated the teacher and interrupted the class, but the students loved it. As a result, Andre's grades plummeted. His popularity soared, however. Now Andre gets all of the attention he once craved.

Unfortunately, young people have very little information about what it means to be Black, and much of that is based on cultural stereotypes. For the most part, those cultural stereotypes do not include Black academic achievement as part of their definition. So as Black children's need to develop friendships and to belong increase, their level of academic achievement typically declines. Being smart is not seen as "cool" among Black children and anyone who shoots for high grades usually does so at the expense of being ostracized. Even those students who do continue to get high grades must usually play down their smarts for continued acceptance among their Black peers.

There is another challenge here. Black students who excel in school have to develop a strategy to be accepted among White students too. Instead of downplaying their smarts, they downplay their Blackness or shy away from anything that might be associated with being Black. This state of "oppositional identity" is when the Black student is on a mission to prove that he is the exceptional Black child and "not like the rest of them." The trouble with this is, no matter how much the Black student assimilates, there are still some people that will always group him with all of the other Blacks and there isn't anything that he can do about it. The difficulty for the student is really not about how others see him; it's more about how he sees himself. As long as he continues to look outside himself for affirmation, he'll never be fulfilled.

The focus for Black children, or Black adults, for that matter, should not be to "fit in," but to make the right fit. As individuals, we need to be confident enough to make friendships with people who share our goals, beliefs, and commitment to success. We should never be in a position to have to minimize any part of ourselves, because authentic relationships should compel us to excel at every level as we develop into our best selves. Who says that academic excellence is exclusively for White people? Although it would be easy to blame our White counterparts for this absurd notion, the fault really lies with us. Some Black parents discourage their children with statements like, "Don't come in here thinking you're better, acting like those White folks." As we move through our communities with low confidence and uncertainty about who we are, it sends the message that success on the educational front doesn't belong to us. It's time that we reclaimed it—for our children and ourselves.

Through my psychological research, I've found that racial identity and self-esteem positively impact academic achievement. When Black children feel confident, have a love for Black people, and have knowledge of their history, they do better academically. What does that mean for us as parents? It means we need to find ways to integrate racial identity and self-esteem at every level of our children's development. By doing this, we're consciously helping our offspring achieve educational excellence, a key factor in ensuring that they realize their potential and fulfill their dreams.

Racial Identity and Self-Esteem: A Winning Combination

A child's assessment of himself, as well as how others assess him, is largely based on how comfortable he feels in his own skin. That's not to say that outsiders don't have their own ideas about race, but our children either validate or invalidate the other person's views. This is an important concept, because it means that we empower our children to influence the future by providing them with the tools of racial identity and self-esteem. As an example, think how your gifted son might respond to his jeering peers if you pointed to the legacy of Black academic achievers as role models; for instance, you could refer to pediatric neurosurgeon Ben Carson, MD.

Historically, Black students who excelled stood as shining examples in their communities and represented hope for the future. Beyond that, it's also important that children know the real consequences of poor academic performance. Janie Victoria Ward, author of *The Skin We're In: Teaching Our Children to Be Emotionally Strong, Socially Smart, and*

Spiritually Connected, says it's important not to pull punches when it comes to talking to children about education. "[P]arents ... need to be brutally honest with their teenagers about the grave consequences of an inadequate education for Black people: poverty, social and political disenfranchisement ... and further marginalization."

Racial identity and self-esteem are not just for parents to emphasize at home. When those factors are properly integrated into the school system, they are even more effective. According to a study conducted by the University of Michigan, students that have racial identity exercises included in their school curriculum get better grades than their counterparts. The study also shows, however, that racial identity must provide the student with a sense of "belonging to a community," not just their "color." For example, the study reported, "an African American student who felt good about being Black and American did well in school. Yet, an African American student who felt good about doing well in school, because it reflected positively on the Black community, excelled, even if he or she viewed society as somewhat racist and against him or her."

In your efforts to build racial identity and self-esteem for academic achievement, assess the institutions and people that are also in your child's life. For example, what type of message is your child receiving from his school about Black academic achievement? What images does he see when he enters the classroom? What does the teacher communicate about Black achievement? What words does the teacher use when describing your child? Sometimes teachers don't even realize they are making unfair distinctions between children. For example, a very active White youngster might be described as "energetic," while the same behavior demonstrated by a Black male of the same age might be seen as "wild." You should also listen for clues from family members. Sometimes their views about race might be inadvertently (or purposefully) imposed upon your child. They may not even know that making references to "good hair" or saying things like "coffee will make you Black," can really hurt a child's self-esteem. It's up to you to assertively, but respectfully, let people know what language you find offensive or, at the very least, unbeneficial to your child's development. While you can't expect others to necessarily agree with you, standing up for your beliefs needs to start with you, if you expect your children to follow suit.

Racial Identity and Self-Esteem Assessment Tool

The previous chapters enabled you to identify specific racial identity and self-esteem issues. Here, we determine whether these factors currently impact your child's academic achievement. Review the following statements to see if they apply to your child, and take notes. Then, continue reading for suggestions on how these issues can be addressed overall. Finally, turn to the chapter that addresses that child's age group for more specific guidelines.

DO ANY OF THE FOLLOWING DESCRIBE YOUR CHILD?
- Doesn't like school
- Poor grades
- Low frustration tolerance
- Class clown; distracts class
- Behavioral problems such as disobedient, disruptive
- Identifies self as stupid
- Doesn't work up to potential
- Avoids doing homework or projects
- Lacks motivation
- Views being smart as acting White

Racial Identity and Self-Esteem at Every Level

At each stage of your child's development, forming racial identity and self-esteem plays a critical role in helping him develop a healthy sense of self and collective belonging. From the time your child is an infant, through adulthood, there are things that you can do to support the development of his racial identity and self-esteem. The next few chapters will specifically outline what actions you should take at each age. There are also things you should do on an ongoing basis. Here are some actions you can take right now:

- **Keep your house filled with educational tools.** In *Achievement Matters: Getting Your Child the Best Education Possible*, author Hugh B. Price says, "Students who have access to an array of reading materials in their homes, including books, magazines, newspapers, and encyclopedias, score higher than those who don't."
- **Go on field trips.** Take your children to museums, bookstores, fairs, and libraries so you can discover the joy of learning together and expose them to culturally sensitive tools.
- **Visit the nursery or school frequently.** This lets the teachers and your children know that you mean business and it keeps them on their toes, since they never know when you'll drop by (just make sure your surprise visits aren't intrusive or counterproductive.). Beyond that, you'll have a better sense of whether the institution you're sending your child to is consistent.
- **Review your child's report card to ensure they're performing at or above grade level.** Request the actual test scores and data and file it away in a safe place. If your child falls below grade level, meet with the teacher to determine how the two of you can bring your child up to speed.

- **Know your child's friends.** I'm not just talking about your child's best friend. Make a point of meeting and knowing your child's classmates, so you can encourage your child to develop relationships with children that share the same values. Also, make a point of meeting with other parents so you can exchange information and see if they also share the same values that you do.
- **Have high expectations for your child.** Find out the requirements for the gifted classes and try to get your child in them. Inspire your child to take rigorous academic courses and encourage your child to take advanced placement courses, even if they're the only African American in the class.
- **Encourage your child to be an achiever.** Celebrate your child's accomplishments and always motivate him to aim for challenging goals. "I believe that children want to do well in the eyes of those adults who are important in their lives," writes Price. "I'm also convinced that when large numbers of them fail, it's mostly because key adults in their lives—parents, relatives, schoolteachers, principals, and their larger community—have failed to nurture them the way we should…"

R.I.S.E., Black Child

Children, at any age, need your protection, nurturing, guidance, discipline and support. However, according to their age and development, certain needs are more critical than others. An infant needs protection and nurturing. A toddler needs to feel safe and protected so that he can learn his environment and gain independence. School-age children need guidance, direction, discipline, and structure. Adolescents need skills that help them transition into adulthood. Although the community, church, educational institutions, and the extended family can be a support system, your participation in your child's development makes a huge difference. Your influence can determine whether your child shoots for the stars or wallows in a pool of self-pity and regret. You truly make the difference.

I know you are up for the challenge. As you study these next few pages, think of ways you can specifically implement these suggestions in your life, so that you and your children can benefit. Also, don't just read the exercises; do them. Your involvement will enable you to become partners in your child's academic success. Let's get started.

Chapter Four: Infants and Babies

What does your baby need from you? At this age, they mainly need to feel safe. This is also the stage where babies first start to experience love as a result of consistent holding, cuddling, and talking to them. Studies show that this type of parent-baby communication is important to your infant's development. Believe it or not, this is also a great stage for you to introduce tools for racial identity and self-esteem development.

How would you do that? It can start just by singing songs and lullabies that reflect African American tradition and heritage. You can also build self-esteem and racial identity as you teach the small things. For example, as you point to different body parts you might say, "These are your beautiful brown eyes. I love your curly brown hair. These are your cute little toes. I love your beautiful brown skin." As babies begin to gain control over their bodies, they will begin to recognize that they can make their arms fling and feet kick. Parents should respond by verbally telling the child what they're doing. By the time the child gets to be six months old, you can start pointing to and verbally identifying their nose, eyes, ears and mouth. Also, smile frequently and you'll notice that your little one will start to smile back at you. These are many different ways to stimulate learning, especially language development.

At this age, the world is a stage for your baby, so he'll expect your constant praise. Give it to him. Praise him for every little thing he does, no matter how small. Clap when he smiles. Cheer when he moves toward something he wants. As your child begins to sit, then crawl, stand, and walk, supervise him but still allow him the freedom of movement and expression. Play games such as peek-a-boo and pat-a-cake to teach social interaction skills. For an Afrocentric twist, dance with your child to the tune of your favorite gospel, jazz, soul or appropriate rap song. You'll not only teach rhythm, balance and coordination this way, you'll also teach your children to dance to the beat of their own drum at an early age.

Spare the Rod

There is no such thing as spoiling a newborn. You can't hold them too much. You can't love them too much. If your baby is crying in the first few months, chances are great that he is truly feeling miserable and needs your comfort. If you pick him up when he cries and that seems to soothe him, it may be that the motion and distraction could have temporarily caused him to forget his tension or pain. A small baby isn't capable of thinking that his every whim is going to be attended to as a result of crying out; he simply lives in the here and now. What he does learn is trust. By responding promptly and lovingly to his cries, you teach him to trust his world, knowing that when problems arise, they will be addressed shortly.

Children at this age should never be spanked. In general, spanking a child at any age should be a last resort. Time-out, a stern look, taking away privileges and redirecting are all better alternatives. Excessive spanking can be as damaging as emotional and verbal abuse. It negatively affects self-esteem. In terms of racial identity, physical control and "beatings" were used during slavery. Black children may perceive themselves as being deserving of physical and harsh treatment, compared to White children. Cross-generational patterns may involve parents learning to use beatings as a way of controlling a child's behavior. This is destructive and abusive. The difference between spanking and beating is the severity and intensity. A parent should also examine his or her motivation. Beating is usually done when a parent is angry and wants to lash out because the child has disrespected or embarrassed him. This type of treatment builds resentment in children. Spanking should be infrequent and done with emotional control by the parent.

Reactions to Strangers

Babies go through many stages when it comes to dealing with strangers. Before the age of six months, your little one can tell if he has seen someone before, but he really doesn't have a reaction to the person one way or another. After six months, children not only recognize people as being familiar or not, they also come to the conclusion that unfamiliar people may be dangerous, and may respond by looking at you and bursting into tears. This is referred to as *stranger anxiety*. To help with this stage, it's okay to keep strangers at bay until your child feels more comfortable in the situation. You can also reassure your child by reacting warmly to the person, especially if the individual is of a different race and your child hasn't frequently been exposed to anyone else of that race.

Despite your child's initial concerns, it's still important that you continue to keep your child around people and in different environments, so that unfamiliar things become familiar. As you do this, don't force your child to interact with anyone that clearly makes her uncomfortable. Like adults, children have their preferences too. Be glad that the stranger anxiety phase generally diminishes at about nine months of age. This is when children realize that even though things may be unfamiliar, they're not necessarily harmful.

Achievement for Babies

We all want brilliant children but we shouldn't get into the habit of pushing a child too early. Sure, you can possibly get your two-year-old to read, but at what expense? Jumping too far ahead in one area almost always results in lagging in another important area. For example, children who learn to read early might have trouble getting along socially. Focusing too much on intellectual development might cause you to miss out on the emotional closeness you should be developing at this stage.

Pressuring a child to learn a skill or to develop a talent is counterproductive. Exposure is best and will lead to knowing what your child's God-given abilities and talents are. Then you can nurture and develop them. This is part of emotional intelligence and includes interpersonal relationships and social interactions.

Also, know that there is no real evidence to indicate that children who "beat" their classmates at learning certain subjects end up any more competent than children who are considered "late bloomers." As Benjamin Spock, MD writes in his book, *Dr. Spock's Baby and Child Care,* "Children develop best when their inborn talents and nature are allowed to blossom at their own pace." Most importantly, be aware that a person's mental ability isn't the only thing required for success. As a parent, you need to also ensure that your children's wits are balanced with common sense, good morals, respect for others, and compassion.

That said, there are some things—baby-friendly things—you can do to stimulate your child's natural cognitive abilities. As long as you don't obsess over these activities, you can begin to set the stage for academic success and cultivate an enthusiasm for learning. Here are some things you can do now:

- **Give your child your undivided attention.** Like you, children can become distracted by interruptions from the television and the telephone. When it's time for quiet time between you and your baby (during a feeding, for example), give your child your undivided attention. Turn the television off and let the answering machine take a message. That lets your little one know, from day one, that your time with him is important. Besides that, quiet time provides a special period for bonding and this sets a precedent for how the two of you will relate to each other for years to come.

- **Read aloud to your children.** Research shows that the critical years for building the foundation for reading and literacy development are from birth to four years old. In your effort to raise children with healthy racial identity and self-esteem, regularly read baby books that feature Black characters and African American folk tales. This lesson will be twofold: 1) it will help your children become better readers themselves, and 2) they'll gain a better appreciation for the material they read, because they are better able to identify with characters that look like them.
- **Talk to your baby.** Even though your baby won't be able to answer you back, at least initially, he'll love the sound of your voice and will learn a lot about language and vocabulary just by hearing you speak. Don't use baby talk because it becomes more difficult for children to learn proper English. It's okay for them to experiment with language later on, but you must ensure that they master the basics first.
- **Encourage your baby to respond back to you.** Using language in a playful manner can inspire expressive communication. "Make up funny-sounding rhymes and silly words," Price suggests. "Infants, toddlers, and young children will be learning all the while as they laugh along with you."
- **Sing lullabies that include racial identity.** Songs are wonderful ways to inspire learning in your babies. The challenge here is that many of the songs we learned as children really don't include Black characters or feature Black stories. Try researching some African American lullabies on your own. Or refer to *Hush Songs* by Joyce Carol Thomas, which contains ten African American lullabies. If you're really feeling inspired, create one of your own. Don't worry about being perfect. Just string

together some lines that will be easy for you to remember and that will have a special meaning for you and your child.

When my daughter, Dotti, first came home from the hospital, I started the practice of singing to her while dressing her. As she got older, she'd sing with me: "I love your beautiful brown hair; I love your smooth Black skin; what lovely brown eyes your have; you are so beautiful to me." As I would sing, I would point to her eyes, nose, ears, toes, etc. Later, Dotti even starting singing the song on her own if I forgot. Although the song never made the Top Ten, it gave me an opportunity to highlight my daughter's unique and special features on a daily basis. This is the foundation of self-image and self-esteem.

- **Start some new traditions and customs that are specially chosen for your own family.** Will you celebrate Kwanzaa? Go Christmas caroling? Or, continue long-standing traditions in which you participated while growing up? The choice is up to you—it really is! As your new family develops, it's your special opportunity to work in traditions that are important to you and your mate. For example, a friend of mine decided to start the tradition of a naming and blessing ceremony for her new son, Jason. Although her family didn't quite understand the purpose when they received the invitations, they were pleasantly surprised when Jill and her husband dedicated a special time to introduce their son to his extended family and friends. The parents took time out to explain the significance of their child's name, tell the meaning of it, ask for blessings from the attendees, and allow each of the guests to hold him. "Although Jason won't remember this time, we'll show him the videotape and pictures to let him know just how loved he was," she explains. At the end of the ceremony, one of the guests made a special song for Jason that the couple hopes to sing at all of their son's special events for years to come. What customs and traditions will your family participate in for years to come? Your selections will help build your child's self-esteem and racial identity.

- **Pray with your baby and for your baby.** It's important to introduce your child to God as early as you can. Start by praying before you go to bed and before meals. Also, take your child to church to worship with you on a regular basis. Teach your child to have a personal relationship with Jesus Christ. When you pray, pray aloud so your child learns how to pray and understands the importance of it. Let your child hear you thank God for him. That's powerful. By doing this, you're not only telling your child how special he is, you're actually showing him.

Chapter Five: Toddlers—Ages 18 Months to 36 Months

Toddlers ask lots of questions because learning is what they do best. As they absorb the world around them, they are curious about how the people in their surroundings agree or disagree with the things they already know about themselves. Be prepared for embarrassing incidents because children at this age have no tact, and they ask questions and make comments based on how they feel in the moment. You can help them in this stage by being sensitive to their innocence and not judging them. Take their comments and responses as they are and don't read anything into them—for now. Just be glad they're still coming to you for the answers because as they get older, that may change.

This stage also puts children on a quest for independence as they develop an increased desire to do things for themselves. This brings with it a toddler's most famous word: "No!" Although this response may be uncomfortable for you at first, know that this phase is a necessary part of his development. By saying "no," your toddler is learning how to decide what he does and does not want. Don't be too hard on your toddler, as far as discipline is concerned. As a parent, you need to allow your child to develop a sense of autonomy and control, because decision-making helps build self-esteem.

How does racial identity mesh with the learning plan for toddlers? It's actually a perfect fit. Quench your toddler's thirst for knowledge by using African American characters, stories, or symbols to illustrate certain points or as part of a lesson. This is also a great time to expose your child to different types of people through playgroups, organizations, birthday parties, and other exciting activities. It's important that your children feel comfortable around people of various racial groups as they navigate the world. It's an exciting time for toddlers as long as you are willing to help them steer, rather than control, the wheel.

Your investigative toddler will be glad you're coming along for the ride.

Safety Measures

As with infants, toddlers still rely on you to make them feel safe. One of the ways you can do that is by trying to build a data bank of positive experiences while minimizing negative ones. Do things to make your toddler feel good. Expose your child to people who will make him feel excited, important, cherished and loved. When visitors come around, let them know how to successfully communicate with your child and encourage your child to interact with people who treat him nicely.

At the same time, shield your child from experiences that are negative, and don't allow your child to interact with people that do or say things to make him cry or hurt his feelings. Sometimes adults can be very rude and nasty to children; don't tolerate it. As a parent, your job is to ensure that your child is protected and you should take that responsibility very seriously, because you are your toddler's only line of defense.

Learn by Example

As your toddler gains better control of his hands, feet, and brain, you'll notice that he'll become quite the imitator. He'll laugh when you laugh. Clap when you clap. He will even get upset when he sees that you are upset. This stage is a good time to put the old saying "practice what you preach" into effect. If you want your child to conduct himself in a respectable manner, you need to behave that way too. If you and your spouse shout at each other as a form of communication, you can expect your two-year-old to soak up that bad habit. At the same time, if you lovingly interact with each other, your youngster will interact with others in the same fashion. Modeling for young children is especially important because they are connecting with the emotions behind your words, since they may not understand what the words actually mean at this point. So be aware of not only what you say when your toddler is around, but also how you say it.

Daycare Beware!

Heart wrenching though it may be, there comes a time when you have to leave your little bundle of joy under someone else's care. A study by the National Center of Education Statistics shows that for half of the mothers in this country, their children are in daycare by nine months of age. The study also found that Black children (69%) are the most likely to be in a daycare when compared to their White (49 %), Asian (47 %), and Hispanic (46 %) counterparts. In addition, Black children are also more likely to spend more than 40 hours a week in a daycare, when compared to White and Hispanic children. These numbers show that it's especially important for *us* to ensure that the people who care for our children in our absence share our values and beliefs.

At the very least, the daycare you choose should be licensed, clean, safe, and have a caring staff. You'll also want to ensure that they have a stimulating curriculum that includes time for group reading, singing, playing solo, physical activities, naps, meals and snacks. A fun-packed day will keep your child joyfully entertained while you're away. Beyond that, you want a daycare center that aids in the development of Black children by offering diversified pictures on the walls, a wide selection of toys and books that include Black characters, and a culturally sensitive staff. That's a tall order but such facilities are out there if you check around. If, for some reason, you can't find one, bring some Black dolls, toys and pictures in yourself—just be sure to use sensitivity when you explain your reasoning to the staff. You might say, "I wanted to bring in some of these items to add to your collection." After that action alone, staff members should understand that you want more racially diverse toys and learning tools within your child's reach. Continue to involve yourself in the daycare facility so that you stay informed and can make adjustments whenever necessary.

When my child was in daycare, I sent her with her Black dolls. Another time, I painted the White Santa Claus on her sweater, brown when I couldn't find a sweater with a Black Santa. I knew I had to do these things because daycare centers generally don't make Black children's needs, as related to Black identity and images, a priority. As the saying goes, the squeaky wheel gets the oil. The more "respectfully" vocal you become about this problem, the more likely you are to resolve the issue.

Cues from Child's Play

You can learn a lot about how children feel about their racial identity and self-esteem by observing how they play with toys, dolls in particular. Toys and dolls help your children explore their imagination and can reveal how they feel about racial differences. My book, *Different and Wonderful: Raising Black Children in a Race-Conscious Society*, was based on my dissertation research, which was a replication of the study by Drs. Kenneth and Mamie Clark, that was used in *Brown vs. the Board of Education*. I discuss how, during a series of interviews, I discovered that many White, as well as Black, children prefer White dolls over Black ones because they perceive them as "prettier," "cleaner," and "nicer." The results of my study concluded that Black children learn at an early age that "Whiteness" is more valued than "Blackness" in this society. As parents, we need to be sensitive to the fact that our children are constantly receiving messages that White is better than Black. As a result, we need to have specific strategies in place to counteract that.

Fortunately, there has been much improvement in Black children's acceptance of Black dolls. If your children happen to prefer White dolls over Black ones, it's important that you show them that Black dolls are beautiful. More importantly, you need to look for opportunities to tell your children about the beauty of Black people. On television, point out the cute brown baby. Or, point to the beautiful models of varying hues in magazines. All of these activities will show your child that Black is beautiful and that's important for the development of his racial identity and self-esteem.

Make Your "Net Work"

Just like you connect with people for job opportunities, you can also talk with them about opportunities for your child. Talk to your colleagues, friends, or family members about recommendations for healthcare, play groups, daycare, and other things you need. If racial identity and self-esteem are important to you, make sure you express that when you ask for a referral. You'd be surprised how much information you can overlook by not tapping the people closest to you.

Milestones to Watch

Initially, your toddler will slowly change his way of communication. From crying, she will move to making gestures and facial expressions, and then to making simple sounds and words. Respond to these actions with lots of cuddling, praise, and talking. Studies report that the more words your child hears by age two, the larger his vocabulary becomes. Introduce your child to a wealth of words and build self-esteem and racial identity by incorporating African American stories, songs and rhymes in your interactions.

Your toddler will also enjoy hearing you tell stories over and over again. Indulge him, as this helps him learn. Also, your little one may surprise you by actually using language to make requests or express his feelings. That's exactly what he's supposed to do: at this point, he is only imitating what he's learned from you so far.

Achievement for Toddlers

This is a very exhilarating time for you and your child. Instead of focusing on the "terrible twos," I believe you'll be able to describe this time as "wonderful," "fantastic" and "amazing," because of all of the positive things you have planned for your youngster. Here are some additional things to add to your "to do" list:

- **Let your child act out.** Yes, let your child use his imagination to act out things that he may have already created in his head. This will give you an idea of what he is thinking, help him learn, and also allow you to participate in this form of play. You can help him restructure the exercise if he does anything that is inappropriate. Psychologists call this technique *projective testing* because children frequently project their feelings and thoughts onto characters they create.
- **Smile in front of a mirror.** Allow your children some mirror time and point out their beautiful Black features while they're doing it. At first, your child may not realize that he is looking at his own image. Once they do recognize themselves, you're in store for even more fun. Don't worry about your child becoming self-centered; children need to be self-centered at this age because this will translate into self-confidence, an essential trait that will help them develop healthy relationships with other people.
- **Take individual and family photos and put them in frames.** Hang them on the wall or put them on a table or dresser for display. This will be a visual for your child that represents your love and pride in him.
- **Hang pictures of Black people in your home.** Let your child see happy, healthy people of color in your own home. Ideally, these photos should be of family

members: sisters, brothers, aunts, and uncles. As they get to know these images, tell your child who they are and what they mean to your family. Don't stop there; also hang pictures of notable African American figures, African art, and other relevant symbols of Black culture.

- **Praise your child for striving for developmental milestones.** Be generous with your hugs, kisses and kind words. No matter how small the accomplishment, let your child know that you're paying attention and encourage him to keep striving.
- **Stress reading.** At this time, start a reading ritual. Get into the habit of reading to your child before you go to work, after you come home, or before your child goes to bed. Read in a comfortable place (e.g. rug, couch, or bed) and sit your child in your lap as you turn the pages. This will help your child make reading a lifelong practice.
- **Bring in the dictionary.** When you use words with which your child is not familiar, tell him what they mean. Then get an age-appropriate dictionary (Afrocentric ones are also available) and show him how to look up the meanings of the words.
- **Bring in the Bible.** This is the perfect time to introduce your child to an age-appropriate Bible. This will communicate the importance of spirituality in your family life. The two of you should read your Bible and pray every day. According to Proverbs: 22:6 (KJV), *"Train up a child in the way he should go: and when he is old, he will not depart from it."*

Chapter Six: Preschool and Kindergarten—Ages Three to Six Years

Issues about race emerge at an early age. Children, whether we acknowledge it or not, are well aware of the physical differences between human beings. Your Black child knows that there is a difference between herself and her classmate Suzie, who has long blonde hair and blue eyes. Beyond that, children also notice differences that exist among Black people. They realize that we come in all different shades, shapes, and sizes. Oftentimes, children at this age will comment on those differences.

This brings to mind a memory of my daughter, Dotti. When she was three years old, she politely told me that it was okay that my skin wasn't as brown as hers and that I was still pretty. It was a good opportunity to talk about different skin tones within the Black race. I felt blessed that she felt good about her skin color and her beauty.

The important thing about dealing with race and young children is how you deal with the questions that they have. Our society often addresses issues of race by ignoring them, overlooking them, or simply not talking about those issues. What people need to realize is that the silence only makes matters worse. When children are silenced, they begin to draw their own conclusions or seek information from the wrong sources. Now that you're able to capture your child's attention, this is an excellent time to share your views about race and how Black people fit in the picture. Of course, the information that you share should be age-appropriate. At the same time, take full advantage of your child's natural curiosity because this is the best opportunity for you to mold them into confident, well-informed African Americans.

Images: Near and Far

When my son, Derek, was three, he would scream out in delight, "Batman! Batman!" when he saw the Batman symbol, or "McDonald's! McDonald's!" when he saw the Golden Arches. Friends would ask, "Did he actually read that?" I would shake my head and reply, "He recognized the symbol. He knows that whenever he sees that symbol, it stands for Batman, or McDonald's."

Yes, children, even at very young ages, start to understand that certain symbols represent other things. Recall the moment that you saw your six-month-old eyeing the bottle, or her mother's breast, because that represented food to her. Even if your preschooler isn't reading yet, you may notice that she'll tell you to "stop" when she sees the octagonal red sign at the end of the street. Or, she'll command you to step on the gas when the light turns green. Perhaps she'll point to the television when she sees her favorite character. Maybe she'll say she is hungry when she sees the Golden Arches. Images have meaning for her.

As a parent, it's your job to determine how your youngster defines Black images and Black people. Has she already taken on the same misconceptions that are so frequently publicized in the media? For example, one of my colleagues commented on her concern about her six-year-old daughter's fondness of Beyoncé, the star of the group Destiny's Child. Apparently, the little girl wanted to copy everything, from Beyoncé's long blonde tresses to the celebrity's very light complexion. The mother wondered whether her daughter was drawn to Beyoncé because of her star power, or because she represented what many African Americans still view as the ultimate Black beauty. In my opinion, my colleague's child was probably influenced by Beyoncé's star power and society's views about beauty. The only way her mother is to know for sure is to ask her daughter about it, and then ensure that she exposes her daughter to other images of beautiful Black women. Women like supermodel Tyra Banks and pop star Janet Jackson, are also versions of attractive African American females. The girl's mother should also showcase photos of the child's grandmother, aunts, cousins and other relatives to let her know that she comes from a long line of beautiful Black women. Use certain images from African art, for instance, to help her love and appreciate her beautiful Black self.

Also, monitor the images that come into your home. A young lady told me that her father forbade them from watching the television show *All in the Family*. "He didn't like racist comments being broadcast in our household, even if they were meant to be jokes," she recalls. Her father's stance communicated a lot about how he felt about bigotry, particularly when it was directed at Black people. You have a responsibility to supervise what images your children see, whether it's over the television, Internet, or some other form of technology. Children form opinions about what they see and you should be there to put those images into the proper context.

Language: Watching Your Words

In looking at images, it's also important for us to make sure that we're not passing on our own biases to our children. For example, do we find ourselves automatically assuming that if we see a Black man running down the street, he stole something? Do we dote more over babies with cream-colored skin than those with hues of pecan brown? Are we still into "good hair" (whether we admit it or not)? Do we describe people using terms like "red bone," "black as tar," "nappy hair," or "high yellow?" All of these things have meaning and they communicate messages to our children: they tell our children how we view ourselves and how they should view themselves. If, out of habit, you do accidentally say something that is inappropriate, you should let your children know that you made a mistake. Group prejudice or racist remarks shouldn't be allowed in your household in any form, even if the comments aren't specifically directed at Black people.

Allow your child to be as verbal and expressive as she wants. In doing this, encourage her to use Standard English. It's not that there is anything wrong with speaking Ebonics, if that's what you choose, but it's important for your children to learn how to speak proper English first. Preschool and kindergarten children love to show off what they know; allow them to show off their speaking ability by encouraging the correct use of their language. Once they master English, then it's okay for them to "switch up," as long as they understand when speaking Ebonics is appropriate.

Milestones to Watch

Diapers, late-night feedings, and potty training are behind you. Now, you have a whole new set of challenges and opportunities ahead of you. ABCs, 123s, story time, mealtime, and snack time will become intimate parts of the days that you and your three-to six-year old share together. These youngsters are asking lots of questions, seeking answers, finding their voice, and noticing the world around them. This includes everything from "Don't Walk" signs to cereal boxes in the supermarket. This is an excellent time for you to make an impression on those impressionable minds.

Preschoolers will be able to identify their letters and begin to understand that words and symbols have meaning. Older children in this group will start to enjoy being read to as they gain a greater understanding of the stories. They'll also like seeing their names in print, as they begin to appreciate the relationship between letters and the sounds they make. Don't disappoint them; encourage their new love of the written word by allowing them to read, draw, or write as much as they'd like.

Achievement for Preschoolers and Kindergarteners

Take advantage of this stage. Learning is fast-paced and it's your job to keep your child on track. Point out labels and signs in her environment. Help kindergarteners identify simple everyday words on signs like "For Sale," "Hospital," "School," "No Smoking," "Caution," "Men's Room," or "Ladies' Room." Make learning fun. As a suggestion, write the new words your child has learned on a Post-It® and put it in her lunch box. Post love notes on the refrigerator or on her mirror. When your child knows that words have special meanings for her, she'll be more interested in learning what they say. This is a good age to help your child practice her writing skills. Most importantly, do whatever you can to pique her interest in learning and discovering.

- **You "name" it.** Put labels on your child's toys, lunchbox, books, clothes and other items. When she sees "Jennifer's mittens," you'll help her expand her vocabulary and help her identify her name.

- **Tell her what her name means.** If your child has an Afrocentric name, then tell her exactly what it represents and post the definition on her bedroom wall as a reminder. Even if the name you chose isn't African, tell your child how you came up with the name and let her know that her name is important. If you convince her of the importance of her name, then she'll know that she must be pretty important in your eyes.

- **Play games.** Start with "I spy with my eye..." as a means to point to various things in her environment. Then, alter the game so that you can begin to incorporate Black leaders, inventors, and objects that have been thoughtfully placed throughout your living space. In addition, play games that build cognitive skills and those that expose children to numbers, the alphabet, shapes, and colors.

- **Keep her moving.** Physical activity is very important

at this age. Try exercises that build motor skills like jumping, skipping, and running. You can also incorporate activities like coloring books, puzzles, and building blocks that aid in fine motor development.

- **Write down her stories.** Seeing her stories in print will build her confidence. She'll also gain an appreciation of how words work together as you help her read her thoughts.
- **Inspire creativity.** Give your child her own personal set of crayons, markers, pencils, and pens, and let her draw to her heart's content. Encourage her to draw people of different racial backgrounds and ask her to point out the "special qualities" in each of her characters.
- **Encourage self-love.** Draw your child as you think she looks, including skin color, hair texture, lips, eyes, and nose. Tell her how pretty she is and how much she is loved. Also allow your youngster to express her imagination by providing her with puppets, dress-up clothes, and stuffed animals. For an Afrocentric twist, incorporate African fabrics, drums and other culturally relevant material during her creative time.
- **Foster emotional exercises.** Allow your child to tell you if she is happy, sad, angry, or frustrated. Help her label her feelings by naming emotions as she expresses them. For example, "You look sad/happy/upset, etc." If she has trouble expressing those feelings, allow her to use dolls to help her communicate. Be very open to discussions about race and African American issues.
- **Ask open-ended questions (not yes or no questions).** When your child responds, show a genuine interest in what she has to say. This exercise will encourage her to tell you what she is feeling, doing, and thinking. You'll build her confidence as she basks in your attention.

- **Get her involved.** Encourage interaction with other children by putting your child in playgroups or taking her to your local library for story time. Also, involve your child in cultural activity groups.

- **Focus on the positive.** Catch your child doing something good and let her know how much you appreciate her for it. Try to ignore minor negative behaviors by simply redirecting your child to what is acceptable and appropriate. Provide lots of praise, attention, and positive reinforcement to increase good behavior.

- **Pray together!**

Side Bar

Ten Signs of a Good Classroom

The National Association for the Education of Young Children (NAEYC) suggests that you look for the following things to ensure that your children (ages 3-6 years old) who attend daycare, preschool, or kindergarten, are involved in a comprehensive learning program:

- **Structured programs:** Children are encouraged to spend the majority of their time playing with materials or other children. They are not expected to sit quietly for long periods.

- **Action-packed:** Children can access materials such as construction paper, building blocks, toys, props, pictures books, paints, games, pegboards, and puzzles to keep them busy throughout the day. Children get bored when they have to play with the same things all of the time.

- **Personal attention:** Instructors are able to work with children on an individual basis and in small groups at different points during the day. The teachers should even read to children on an individual basis, in addition to reading to the group. It's important that your child has some one-on-one time.

- **Culturally sensitive:** The classroom should be decorated with African American items of interest, along with the children's

original artwork and other creations.
- **Creative learning techniques:** Children should learn the alphabet and numbers through interaction with things in the environment and by participating in interesting activities. For example, children can learn their numbers by counting the animals or plants, or by taking attendance. They can also learn by cooking, handing out supplies, or assisting the instructor.
- **Exploration encouraged:** Children should be allotted at least one hour to work on projects, play and explore. Worksheets shouldn't be the most popular tool used.
- **Outdoor time:** Weather permitting, children should play outside on a daily basis. Instructional time is no substitute for outdoor play.
- **Comprehensive curriculum:** Lessons should be adapted so that they meet the needs of the children who are ahead, as well as for those who need additional help. Teachers need to be sensitive to the different abilities and experiences of their students.
- **Peace of mind:** Both you and your children should be comfortable with the school's environment. If your child doesn't seem excited about attending the program, find out why and look for another option.
- **Seal of approval:** Find out if the program is accredited by NAEYC, which proves that it meets a standard of excellence in early childhood education.

For a free brochure, "Good Teaching Practices for Older Preschoolers and Kindergartners," send a stamped, self-addressed, business-size envelope to NAEYC, Box 522, 1509 16th Street, N.W., Washington, DC 20036.

Chapter Seven: School-Age Children

Children between the ages of seven and twelve are in a special time in their lives. Although their parent's influences are still important, now friends, classmates, teachers and other people at school play a major role in their development. Children in this age group are particularly sensitive to racial concerns and how it impacts their world. An author recalls her first memories surrounding this issue:

> I was eight years old the day my mother warned me not to play in the sun, and I already knew that I was invisible. I had not read Ralph Ellison's Invisible Man. Toni Morrison had not yet written The Bluest Eye. But already I had tasted the essence of racial and colorist tragedy. I feasted on it every day. I had parents who loved me, a nurturing family, many friends. I was smart in school, was often considered the teacher's pet. And I also knew that the specific physical traits that comprised my racial identity were despised.
>
> Words had informed me of this. The words from family and friends that showered praise and compliments on lighter-hued, straighter-haired children for their beauty, words that I never heard used to describe brown to black children. Words like, "Isn't she so pretty?" uttered with a sharp intake of stunned breath, eyes bulging in near-disbelief, at the sight of a curly-haired, light-skinned toddler. Words like, "Just look at that hair!" (Translation: it was long, straight, thick.)
>
> Marita Golden
> Author, *Don't Play in the Sun*

In dealing with your youngster, choose your words carefully, especially when it comes to discussions about race. As discussed earlier, self-esteem and racial identity have a direct influence on your child's educational achievement. In other words, children who feel good about themselves, as individuals and as African Americans, will do better in school. At the same time, Black students who lack these essential characteristics are less likely to achieve academic success. Since they don't believe in themselves, they spend less time studying and applying themselves and are more focused on their perceived shortcomings than on their positive qualities. Your comments, such as, "don't play in the sun because you'll get too dark," for example, could do irreparable damage to your youngster's personal and academic success, both over the short- and long-term.

In fact, research suggests that things get worse over time, not better. Students who do poor academically typically fall behind at every grade level. That's why it's important that you deal with any issues your child might have with self-esteem and racial identity, sooner rather than later.

Teachers: The Role They Play

Teachers, who spend a large part of the day interacting with our children, have a significant impact on their self-esteem (whether they know it or not). In most cases, a child's failure in a particular area may have more to do with the child's "perceived" potential in that area, rather than his "actual" potential. To put it simply, if you see yourself as incompetent, then your performance will probably reflect that view. It's up to teachers to show all of their students that they can succeed, and then provide them with the tools to actually do it.

In an online article, one teacher/child psychologist found that his role in the classroom was paramount to student success. Ham Ginott observed:

> *I've come to the frightening conclusion that I am the decisive element in the classroom. It is my personal approach that creates the climate. It is my daily mood that makes the weather. As a teacher, I possess a tremen-*

dous power to make a child's life miserable or joyous. I can be a tool of torture or an instrument of inspiration. I can humiliate or humor, hurt or heal. In all situations it is my response that decides whether a crisis will be escalated or de-escalated and a child humanized or dehumanize.

It's unfortunate that all teachers don't feel as strongly as Ginott does about their influence on their students. When teachers lower their expectations of their students, display negative attitudes and/or biases toward them, discourage their participation, and publicly humiliate them, they directly contribute to the failure of those students. In contrast, when teachers focus on the strengths of those students, build their confidence, as well as highlight the unique contributions each pupil makes to the classroom, those teachers facilitate high academic achievement in the classroom. This is true of both Black and White teachers.

Research suggests that there are certain methods that teachers and schools can use to help Black students learn. African American children benefit from direct teacher contact and smaller classroom sizes. In fact, in a 1985 Tennessee study that tracked students for ten years, it was found that although White students placed in smaller classrooms at an early age performed slightly better on math and literacy exams than White students in regular classes, African Americans performed much better when taught in smaller classroom sizes.

When you make your school selection, consider the questions in the sidebar that follows and ensure that your child's teacher has high expectations for all of her students (including African Americans). Ideally, try to get your child in a classroom that has fifteen students or less. Do as much as you can to ensure that your child is put in an environment that will help—not hinder—his academic achievement.

Standardized Testing

Although standardized testing has been around for some time, the issue has been under additional scrutiny since the No Child Left Behind Act became law in 2003. Under this law, schools, districts, and states are given a report card based on the results of standardized tests. These assessments, which also evaluate test scores by race, have found gaps at every level. This has put educators on the hunt for the answer to a burning question: *Why do Black students score significantly lower on standardized tests than their White counterparts?*

Researchers have come up with two major reasons: 1) predominately Black schools, which lack funds for the extra expenses they incur for counseling, healthcare, and special education, aren't considered when monies are distributed; and 2) teachers—even Black teachers—fail to acknowledge their own biases when it comes to student performance; they also don't appreciate how much Black students are affected by what others think of them (an observation referred to as *stereotype vulnerability*). These factors lead to very different results for Black and White students, even if they are within the same classroom.

Of course, identifying the problem is only part of the solution. It's not likely that politicians, educators, or the parents of children in predominately White schools would agree that funds be redirected to predominately Black schools because they have greater needs in certain areas. Additionally, teachers who don't think they contribute to the performance gap aren't likely to do anything to change their behavior. The teachers' unions and education boards often cite the achievement gap as a class issue, and so there is no pressure for teachers to reassess their teaching techniques.

In any case, don't let your child be victimized by standardized tests. Although these tests do indicate past or future achievement, they do not adequately measure intelligence. If you have an issue with standardized testing, exercise your right to secure independent outside testers. Also realize that your child will be assessed by the scores on these tests. You may want to get your child the extra help that he needs to succeed by enrolling him in summer courses or signing up for specialty testing training courses.

Black Boys and the School System

The educational system is failing our Black boys, yet there has been no national commitment to resolve this widespread problem. Researchers say that the first signs of trouble emerge when African American boys reach the third or fourth grade. Prior to that, Black males perform on par with boys and girls of all races on standardized math and reading tests. By the third or fourth grade, there is a sharp decline in the way African American boys perform, according to the National Center for Education Statistics.

Why do Black boys have particular difficulty when they reach eight or nine years old? There seems to be a shift in teaching methods that rubs our sons the wrong way. In the earlier years, socializing is encouraged but that environment changes as the children get older. The interactive "learn by doing" format is transformed to a "sit down and listen" structure. That atmosphere is toughest on our sons, who tend to be very energetic. In addition, tension tends to build between Black male students and their teachers (White or Black), who may actually fear them. When that occurs, any act of defiance (no matter how small) can aggravate an already volatile situation; that's how many Black boys are inappropriately labeled "problem children" very early in life.

Unfortunately, the problems that Black boys encounter at this early stage are only the beginning. Many of our sons are in store for a long line of failures. In 2000-1, Black boys made up only 8.6 percent of national public school enrollments but were over-represented in the following problem areas:

- **Special Education:** Black boys constituted 20 percent of mentally retarded students, 21 percent of emotionally disturbed students, 12 percent of students with specific learning disabilities, and 15 percent of special education students. Black boys are twice as likely to be in special education than Black girls.

- **Expulsions and Suspensions:** Black boys make up 22 percent of school expulsions and 23 percent of school suspensions.

- **Dropouts:** The dropout rate for African American males in many metropolitan areas is 50 percent.

- **Graduation Rates:** Nationally, only 50 percent of Black males receive diplomas with their high school classmates.

- **Juvenile Incarceration Rates:** There are more Black youths in prison than in higher education facilities or the military.

These problems are too significant to ignore. As a community, we need to commit resources to ensure that the Black boys in our community succeed. As parents, you need to be actively involved in your son's life in order to catch problems early, and you should be particularly sensitive to your child's attitude toward education as he enters the third and fourth grades. You should know what your child is supposed to learn at each grade level, ensure that the teacher is covering that material, and do what you can to ensure that your child grasps the concepts. Parents need to have the same mindset as teachers: have high expectations for your sons and they'll meet or exceed those expectations.

There are many high-achieving Black boys whose accomplishments go unnoticed. The achievement test scores of my nephew, Julian Garlington, were on a high school level when he was in the sixth grade. My son, Derek, accelerated a grade and will start high school when he is twelve years old. Derek's best friend, Shawn Robinson, demonstrated academic excellence by being accepted into an exclusive independent school. Shawn is a freshman in high school and encourages Derek. There are many Black boys with similar achievements in your community. We need to praise them and recognize their hard work. There is a national program that parents should look into, called Granville Academy. The program has a branch in Waterbury, CT, which is run by attorney Maurice Mosley. He does a phenomenal job in providing youth with academic enrichment, college preparation, cultural awareness, and exposure to Historically Black Colleges and Universities (HBCUs). Black youth, especially males, need programs that are affirming and enriching.

White Schools versus Black Schools

In 2004, we celebrated the fiftieth anniversary of the Supreme Court's landmark decision in *Brown v. Board of Education,* where it was determined that "separate but equal" has no place in the educational system. Supposedly, this law outlawed segregation, but did it really? Today, more than 7 out of 10 Black students attend predominantly minority schools. Though Whites make up only 60 percent of public school children, most have little contact with minority students, except in the South and Southwest.

Not only are the majority of public schools separate—as far as race is concerned—they remain unequal. As pointed out earlier, there is a significant achievement gap between White and Black students, where African Americans lag significantly on standardized tests. One study, from the Educational Trust, found that "by the end of the fourth grade, African American, Latino and low income students are already two years behind grade level...by the time they reach the twelfth grade they are four years behind." Also stated earlier, insufficient funding of Black schools largely contributes to this disparity. This leaves some Black parents with the tough decision of whether they should sacrifice the culture afforded by Black schools for the educational opportunities provided at White schools.

As I pointed out in my book, *Different and Wonderful: Raising Black Children in a Race-Conscious Society*, most predominately White schools have a strong economic base that affords for a higher-quality education than sparsely funded Black schools. If you want to take advantage of these school offerings, its important that you expose your child to Black culture by involving him in outside activities such as Boy Scouts, church, and sports. In addition, it's important to provide your child with a number of African American role models so that he becomes familiar with Black success.

On the other hand, if you choose to keep your child in a predominately Black school, be honest about the education that it provides so you can actively find academic enrichment programs. At the same time, allow your child to indulge in all the culture the school has to offer as it relates to dance, music, hairstyle, dress and history. Just remember to assess your child's Black school by the same standards that you'd use to judge any other educational program.

My children have experienced the good and bad of both environments. Unfortunately, it may be a challenge to find the best system, especially in certain parts of the country. Don't become disillusioned. Continue to be positive and proactive in finding the best environment for your child. Ideally, magnet schools and well-integrated schools offer the best of both worlds: academic excellence and cultural diversity.

> **Side Bar**
>
> What you need to consider when selecting your child's school:
> - Can my child's school teach a culturally changing student body?
> - Will the school prepare my child to succeed in a culturally diverse society?
> - Does the school's values conflict with the ones I am teaching at home?
> - How open is the school to my suggestions?
> - Do I have a good relationship with the teachers and other faculty? (If no, do I think I can successfully develop a relationship?)
> - How important is a multicultural education to me?

Milestones for School-Age Children

You have a lot to look forward to during this phase of your child's life. Initially, your six- or seven-year-old will start to read his own books and retell the stories in his own words. Then he'll write about meaningful topics, use punctuation and capitals in his writing, and read books that are designed for his age with little difficulty. During the next years, he will expand his vocabulary and even use the proper language rules when he's writing or speaking. You may also notice that he'll correct his own mistakes, and yours, as he begins to feel more confident. As he gets older, you'll enjoy his full-fledged book reports, poems and stories. If you have a speller on your hands, you'll enjoy your child's participation in his school's annual spelling bee.

At this age, Black children are sensitive to fair play, as they are fine-tuning their value system, sense of rules, and conscience. It's not uncommon for children at this age to complain because they are mistreated or believe they are victims of prejudice or discrimination. Your child may tell you that they've been teased by another child for being "too light," "too dark," "having too big of a backside," "having nappy hair," "having White girl hair," "talking ghetto," or "talking White." All of these comments can be very confusing to a child. As a parent, you should listen and remain calm without projecting your own experiences onto your youngster. If the issue isn't severe, the child may work the problem out himself.

If your child has difficulty working out the issue, you need to intervene by talking with the parent of the other child, the teacher, or a school official. Use it as an opportunity to foster acceptance of differences. Conflict resolution skills will help defuse the situation and teach positive social skills. Role play appropriate responses with your child. Create conflict situations and have your child act out how she would respond. Teach and guide her in what to say and how to say it assertively. Discourage aggressive responses that escalate the conflict. Also, discourage passive responses that allow your child to be a victim.

Achievement for School-Age Children

When it comes to improving self-image, self-esteem, and racial identity, accomplishment is key. Ensure your children are involved in a learning environment that promotes praise, encouragement, and opportunities for success, and they'll continue to have a positive self-image. On the flip side, children who become frustrated because they don't see opportunities for achievement will experience damage to their self-image. Worse yet, when children fail to achieve in school, they often look outside of school for affirmation and are drawn to illegal activity or other forms of self-destructive behavior. It's your job to identify negative influences before they have a chance to impact your child's life.

As a parent, you still have a big influence over your child's success. This is because positive self-esteem and a high degree of racial identity are a result of his home experiences. Still, it's important for you to know that this is also the stage where much of what you say may start to take a backseat to what his peers and teachers say and do. It's all part of the process of your child separating himself from the family and claiming his own place in the world. Here are some things that you can do to help him make this transition:

- **Organize activities.** Children at this age like games with structured rules that require skill. They are interested in activities like hopscotch, jump rope, jacks, and video games. This is also the time to get them involved in hobbies like sports card collecting, because they're old enough to start arranging things in an orderly fashion.
- **Reward them.** Provide them with intrinsic rewards by using praise and recognition for schoolwork to instill self-pride. Also give extrinsic rewards, like small gifts or trips to the movies.
- **Nurture independence.** Children at this age want to be treated as individuals who are less dependent on their parents. They even turn to trusted adults that are outside of the family for advice. It's not that they've forgotten the lessons from Mom and Dad, but they've made them their own creations at this point. Try not to remind him about the rules as much because you're sure to hear, "I know that already," as a sign that he's being independent.
- **Nip bad manners in the bud.** In an effort to declare his

independence, you may notice your child displaying habits that make you unhappy. Your previously well-behaved "pumpkin" might do naughty things like forget table etiquette, absentmindedly kick the table leg, slam the door, or leave his coat lying around. As with younger children, try to influence his behavior by redirecting your child to what is acceptable and appropriate.

- **Start an allowance.** This will show your child how to manage money as well as inspire him to develop constructive ways to earn cash. You should allow your child to buy whatever he wants with his allowance as long as he isn't breaking any household rules, like excessive candy or toy guns (if you happen to be against them).
- **Encourage your child to write to relatives in a different city.** This will help him improve his reading and writing skills, as well as learn about family heritage.
- **Involve children in sports as well as community and cultural activities.** Participation in sports will help your child improve physical stamina, develop an appreciation for teamwork, and improve his social skills. Other activities like African drumming and dance, for example, will help your child gain a great appreciation for his community and will strengthen his racial identity.
- **Stress reading.** Fill your home with magazines, books, newspapers, and other reading material, particularly if they are related to African Americans or our history. Go to the library regularly and have your youngster fill out his own application for a library card. Show him how to read a hymnbook, map, recipe card, bus schedule, graph, or information on Black history. All of these things communicate that reading is important in your household.
- **Tell your child about God's gift and purpose for our lives.** This is important as your child develops a rela-

tionship with God. Outside forces will have less influence over his moral character, self-image, and self-esteem. A child who knows God is able to be open to God's guidance. This helps him learn the details of his God-given gifts. In addition, prayer and talking to God teaches him how to deal with life's challenges and adversity.

Chapter Eight: Adolescence—Thirteen Years of Age and Older

Welcome to your child's time of self-discovery. At this age, hormones are raging as teens begin to experience biological processes that inspire some very visible physical changes. Girls grow breasts and pubic hair. Boys grow facial and pubic hair, their voices change and they may shoot up in height. From a psychological viewpoint, this stage may come with confusion as teenagers begin to explore the questions of "Who am I?" and "What will I become?" Black teens, in particular, have the added pressure of determining "What does being Black really mean?" As parents, it's our job to help them answer their questions and ease our youngsters' volatile transitions from children to adults.

Some very real things happen during puberty that compels your teen to classify herself by race. First, schools tend to sort children based on ability around this time. Generally, Black children are grouped into the slower track while their White counterparts are moved into Honors programs or more accelerated classes. Next, the outside environment also changes as parents become increasingly concerned about race mixing for older children. While it may have been okay for five-year-olds of various backgrounds to socialize, parents get nervous when Black and White teenagers mix. As a result, adolescents begin to separate at school and in social settings. Lines in the sand are drawn.

How does your youngster feel about the changing environment, and how does this affect her attitudes about her self-worth? It all depends on the messages she has received. In this stage, you'll begin to see how your attitudes, impressions, and conversation helped shape her view of race and her own racial identity. It really is a case of reaping what you've sown.

Positively (or Negatively) Black

Sixteen-year-old Lee was a huge rap fan. As he pumped up the volume of the radio in his room, his mother nearly hit the roof when she heard the words to the song "99 Problems." She ferociously knocked on the door and demanded that Lee "turn that trash off." Lee didn't see the big deal. After all, that wasn't the first time he'd heard the B-word. His father called his mother that whenever he got upset with her, and his mother cursed more than any rap artist. "You're such a hypocrite," Lee yelled back. Despite the mother's disappointment with Jay-Z's lyrics, she couldn't argue because her son was right. "Then would you at least turn it down?" she asked; she felt that was the only compromise available.

The mother above is not alone. Sometimes we are caught by surprise when we discover the influences that shape our children's views about Black people, especially when those views come from us. It's important that you find out whether or not your child is internalizing the negative propaganda that circulates about African Americans. If not, can you pinpoint what messages you have sent that helped her create such a positive self-image? At the same time, if your teen has some real issues with her Blackness, you should also take a hard look at the examples that you've set as far as race is concerned. Look at the behaviors you've demonstrated in your home. Do you and your spouse fail to treat each other with respect? Do you fail to treat your children with respect? Do you speak negatively about other Black people? Do you watch television shows or listen to programs that degrade a group of people (whether it be women, men, Black people or anyone else)? It's really difficult to influence your adolescent's behavior if you're not setting a good example. Adolescents have a strong sense of fairness and are judgmental of adults and peers that they consider unfair.

Know that the majority of what she has learned about race, and where Black people fit into the world, came from you. Still, as she continues to interact with her peers, teachers, and other educators, these views could change. Just hope that she'll include you in her struggles as she tries to sort things out.

You'll see her sense of style emerge. She'll either conform to the preferences of her classmates—which may be the safest route but not necessarily the best one—or she'll create a look of her own. Just know that adults tend to be more hesitant in accepting new styles but if you absolutely hate her choice, you may win her over by respectfully explaining your objection and persuading her to make another selection. On the other hand, you may be in for a fight. As you take issue, be aware that there were some parents who absolutely hated the platform shoes and bell-bottom pants that were so popular in their day. Just as they did when you were growing up, your child's clothing picks provide her with a sense of self-expression.

No Time for Kidding

"Stop treating me like a kid!" children exclaim in response to your expression of concern about their whereabouts, or insistence that they button up their sweater all the way to the top. You know you're trying to protect them but they feel as if you're trying to stifle their adult development. They're rebelling against many of the norms that you've put in place, in an effort to maintain their individuality and grow. As hard as it is, it's time to let them make some decisions for themselves. That also means allowing them to live with some of the consequences of the decisions they make. That's the cost of independence.

It's also important to let your teen know that although you understand the physical and emotional changes she's going through, other adults may not. This may be tough to explain because similar behavior in White teens might be seen as "a phase," while Black teens are often viewed as being overly aggressive or even dangerous whenever they exhibit any behaviors that make other people uncomfortable. That's why it's particularly important that Black teens (Black boys, especially) learn self-control and exercise as much caution as possible during this stage. Otherwise, they could put themselves at risk for police aggression or inappropriate retaliation from teachers or other professionals.

Peer Relations

Although you may hold the answers to many of their questions about race, chances are your child won't come to you for them. She's more interested in what her friends have to say about the matter. She'll look to them for cues on how to be Black, how to act Black and how Black people fare when compared to other races. Unfortunately, much of the information that her friends rely upon is based on stereotypes and misinformation that have been perpetuated by White people.

Among adolescents, certain speech, music, dress, and other characteristics are classified as "authentically Black." Black boys roam the streets with clothes in certain colors and styles, and Black girls will take on certain attitudes, as evidence that they belong to a group that appreciates them and affirms their racial identity. These children share a group of norms, values, and experiences that help them relate and support each other. As long as the group is not involved in any negative activity—drugs or crime, for example—it plays a very important role in your youngster's development.

Milestones for Adolescents

At this stage, your adolescent may be coming to terms with his new physical self as he begins to appreciate his gender (also known as *gender identity*). You should also notice your teen becoming more responsible as he manages his own school schedule, chores, and can travel away from the nest on his own. In addition, your teen's growing need for financial self-sufficiency might motivate him to express desire for a job or ask that you set up a bank account for him. Take him along when you set up the bank account, or assist him in filling out applications, so that he can have a guideline for future reference.

Academic Achievement for Adolescents

It's unfortunate that of the many personas African Americans teens take on, none seem to include academic achievement. Succeeding on the educational front is seen as "acting White." As teens begin to cling to racial identity as a means to separate themselves from anything that might be associated with being White, their academic performance suffers.

It's important that parents let their teens know that Blacks historically valued education. You can also point to key figures in Black history and among your family tree that demonstrate this. In addition, there are other guidelines you can put in place to prevent your inquisitive teen from wandering too far out of bounds:

- **Set boundaries.** Teenagers can be rude, loud, disrespectful, angry, disobedient and downright annoying. If you find that your teenager is out of hand, let him know that the behavior is unacceptable and won't be tolerated. You can say, "Don, I will not talk to you while you're screaming. You will not talk to me in that way. When you change your tone, we can have a conversation." Although they'll never admit it, children know that parents set rules because of a deep love and desire to protect their offspring.
- **Practice the Golden Rule.** When dealing with adolescents, you should treat them as you wish to be treated.

Listen to their feelings and ideas. Give them some flexibility by allowing them to negotiate on things like curfews, style of dress, hairstyles, and friendships. That's not to say you shouldn't express your discontent about something, but do so in a respectful manner that allows the child to have some influence on the final decision.

- **Keep it moving.** As children progress through grade levels, they may fulfill their physical education requirements early on and may not have to take any additional courses that keep them active. That's not good, because exercise is very important at this age. It enables children to maintain their energy, manage their weight and even boost their mood. Exercise increases the production of endorphins, which are the "feel-good" hormones.

- **Safeguard their privacy.** Teens need their privacy and it's important that you respect that in order to avoid unnecessary conflict. Not only should you not snoop around in their room, book bag or other belongings, you should also refrain from telling other people about your teen's personal issues. When you keep their secrets, you build trust and that creates an opening for them to communicate with you in the future. The exception is when you see signs that your child is doing something that is harmful, like drugs. In cases like this, the privacy rule is out. It is your home and you have the right to be intrusive when it comes to your child's safety and health.

- **Encourage open dialogue about sexual development.** The best relationship with your teen is when the two of you can talk openly about sexual development and you are able to guide him or her. Practice being an open listener without being judgmental or "preachy." Encourage youth to share more. Allow your son or daughter to talk about his or her perceptions of other teens, peers, and friends. Once your teen has been able to share, disclose and ask questions, then you can provide guidance and direction.

- **R-E-S-P-E-C-T.** Males and females should be taught to not only respect their bodies but to respect the opposite sex. Misogynistic messages in the media, particularly rap music, can affect our children's images and views of Black people's sexuality. This should be pointed out and discussed. Many teens are able to distinguish between images and reality, therefore viewing it as entertainment and not something to be expressed in everyday life. Teaching self-respect, respect for others, and positive images helps to develop healthy sexual relationships at the appropriate time. Young Black males and females should be taught abstinence. However, knowing about protection and safe sex is essential for those who decide to be sexually active.
- **Advocate sexual health and access to health services.** Speaking of health, know that your teen may seek confidential medical care because she may not want you to know she's sexually active. Although that's not an ideal situation, it's better that your teen opts for good medical care than none at all. Sexuality is connected to racial identity and self-esteem. Black youth need guidance in understanding that sexuality is a normal and healthy part of human development.
- **Encourage healthy sexual self-esteem.** Dressing in a manner that is flattering and has sex appeal is not the same as dressing like you are in a BET music video. Self-image and positive self-esteem enable youth to make wise choices about how they dress and want to be perceived. Peer influences will certainly

impact this, and your job as a parent is to temper these influences with the boundaries you've established with your child. Explain to your teen why you do or do not object to certain articles of clothing. Give her room to make the proper choices, so that she won't feel an overwhelming need to sneak behind your back.

- **Permit on-the-job training.** It's not uncommon for teens, from the age of fourteen on up, to get their first job. This can be a positive experience because it allows them to meet other teens, earn their own money and demonstrate responsibility. At the same time, parents should monitor the experience to make sure that their child isn't working too hard, ignoring their homework, or missing out on valuable sleep. It is a federal law that children who are in school full-time can only work a maximum of twenty hours per week during the school year. Also, be aware of the safety and health risks associated with some jobs and supervise your teen accordingly.
- **Encourage their participation in the upkeep of your home.** By now, your child should have chores that he either completes in a timely fashion or deals with the consequences for not completing those tasks. Having household responsibilities provides your child with a sense of dignity, pride, and responsibility because he knows that he is making a necessary contribution to the family's well being.

Chapter Nine: The Role of Family

What is a family? It depends on whom you ask. In White society, most view the *nuclear family* as the norm. It consists of a mother, father, and a child (or children). In our community, we belong to an *extended family*, which not only includes the parents and siblings but also grandparents, aunts, uncles, and even family friends. Since Black people generally believe it takes a village to raise a child, anyone who might be directly involved in the child's development is considered family.

The extended family, however, is changing for the Black community. Although it continues to be a source of strength, it has diminished in significance. In the past, many "extended" family members lived in the same community, so it was easier to communicate and support one another. Today, families may be spread out across the country so the members can't provide the same daily emotional and material support that they have in the past, and the Black family is feeling the effects.

Now, the Black family has become far less structured. Today, only one-third of Black children grow up in a two-parent home. Black children are half as likely as their White counterparts to live in a two-parent household and are eight times more likely than White children to have an unwed mother as a parent. Most Black children under six years of age live with a mother who was never married.

Strengths of the Black Family

So what does that mean for parents today? It means we have to design our children's lives so they still get the benefits of the extended family. In my book, *Different and Wonderful*, I highlighted the five major strengths of the Black family as identified by researcher Robert Hill in his book, *The Strengths of the Black Families*. Although I still believe these strengths need to be celebrated and maintained, I also think we need to determine how to make them work in our families as they exist today. Here's a look at how these strengths might be considered:

- **Strong Kinship Bonds:** This refers to the members in our extended family that help raise, influence, and love our children. This includes our grandparents, aunts, uncles, and family friends. As pointed out, our extended family members aren't as likely to be in close proximity as they were in the past; it's up to the parents to develop a specific plan so that their children can maintain strong relationships with their relatives and other guardians. This is especially important in families where the parents aren't together or aren't married, because children need a variety of positive, encouraging people in their lives to hold them accountable and to serve as role models.

- **Adaptability of Family Roles:** Traditionally, the Black family has been far more flexible than their White counterparts when it comes to division of labor and who brings home the bacon. For the most part, both parents worked outside of the home. Since Black women are now the primary heads of household as single parents, there needs to be even more flexibility as far as roles are concerned. Children may have to take on more responsibility or the mother may have to bring other people in the household to help with chores. The main thing is for there to be openness to new solutions that will help the household run more effectively and efficiently.

- **Strong Work Orientation**: Black families have always had a very strong work ethic. To continue this tradition, it's important that children maintain an appreciation for what their parents do. That's why programs like Take Your Daughter/Son to Work Day are so very important. Children get a firsthand look at their parent's work environment and can decide whether or not they'd like to consider a similar career. To take this a step further, switch off with other parents—whether they're other family members or friends—each year so that your children get to see a variety of work settings.

- **Strong Educational Achievement Orientation:** African Americans know the value of a good education but as society continues to become more competitive, it's important for us to ensure that our children get an excellent education. You do that by getting involved in the educational process and ensuring that your child's school is offering the appropriate curriculum in an environment that is culturally sensitive. If your child's school falls short, insist that the district transfer your youngster to a stronger public school.
- **Strong Religious Orientation**: The church continues to be a strong influence in the Black family. Although the traditional Black family structure is changing, as more women become single parents, the church can help bridge the gap for children who grow up without fathers. Involving your children in church activities can provide them opportunities to develop leadership skills, socialize with their peers, and connect with strong male and female role models.

All of these strengths help our children develop strong self-esteem and racial identity, which will ultimately contribute to academic achievement. It's important that we understand, and help our children understand, that despite the many things that plague us, we can rely on the strength of our own families to help us find the solutions.

Family Assessment Tool

Are you ready to evaluate your family's strengths? Please

review the following inventory guide, make copies for members in your extended family, and have each of you fill it out while you're together. Once everyone is ready to share their results, host a discussion about how you all can make the family even stronger.

VO = Very Often
O = Often
S = Sometimes
NO = Not Often
N = Never

	VO	O	S	NO	N
Plans family activities					
Discusses family problems					
Protects and supports each other					
Shows affection					
Has responsibility for each other					
Expresses feelings openly					
Attends each other's activities					
Confides in each other					
Cries with each other					
Confronts each other					

Chapter Ten: The Role of School

It's time we raised the bar. Academic failure should not be an acceptable option for our youth and we should do whatever we can to ensure that our schools put our children squarely on a path for success. Fortunately, many schools are already doing a great job, but a large proportion of them fall short. Where that's the case, it's our responsibility to pressure educators, lawmakers, community leaders, and state politicians to make improvements.

Some of the new developments we should insist on are 1) a redistribution of funds so that schools who need the most resources (those in poor Black neighborhoods) actually get the funds; 2) a response to school report cards. It's just not enough to know how your child's school compares to others in the district; you should also receive a written explanation of what the school plans to do in the future to increase it's rating; 3) more one-on-one student/teacher contact to facilitate individual attention; 4) an incorporation of positive African American literature and images in the classroom to raise students' racial identity and self-esteem; and 5) any other activities educators believe will improve academic achievement among Black students.

On a broader scale, Congressman Jesse Jackson, Jr. is pushing to amend the United States Constitution as a means of ensuring that quality education becomes a right for all Americans. By doing this, education would be taken from state jurisdiction and be put under federal rule, forcing the educational system to become a unified, standard system from state to state. For minorities and low-income Americans, this would be ideal. According to Jackson, if education is made an inalienable right, like life, liberty and the pursuit of happiness, Blacks could then legally demand that their state bring their schools on par with the nation's best schools. Although a national educational restructure isn't something that could happen overnight, the congressman says that amending the Constitution is the first step. In the meantime, Jackson also encourages African Americans to continue the fight for quality education on a local level.

Teachers Can Make a Difference

In 1999, one woman received her first teaching assignment. The young White recent graduate was placed at the Prescott Elementary School in Oakland, California. She was thrilled with her new position, especially since it was at Prescott. The school was receiving a lot of media attention because of its reputation for high achievement among African American students and adoption of an "Ebonics" program. Her colleagues, however, were not as enthusiastic. They warned her that the students and faculty at Prescott "hate White people." They thought a newcomer would be met with hostility, defiance, and disrespect.

This teacher's experiences were to the contrary. Although it was clear by the school curriculum, pictures on the walls, the books in the library, and assembly calendar that African American history and achievement were central to the school, it was also evident that the students and the faculty had an appreciation for people of all cultures. There were also specific activities that celebrated the achievements of Mexicans and Cambodians, in order to address the needs of those students.

Veteran teachers not only welcomed her, they offered ideas and resources to help with her lesson plans. "I had found my home," she says, as she recalls those first few days at Prescott. She specifically pointed out that the Ebonics rumors were misconceptions. Even though teachers respected students' home cultures by allowing them to speak Ebonics throughout the school, the teach-

ers were also required to help the students translate their home language to Standard English in the classroom. Most importantly, this enlightened newcomer says that the teachers at Prescott saw themselves as part of the community and were committed to helping students identify with their heritage through positive images and affirmation. "This was the kind of teaching that I longed to do, and I was relieved that I had found a place where it was not only going to be safe to do it, but it would also be valued and accepted. I couldn't believe my luck."

The teacher above is a prime example of the important role that teachers play in the educational system. Despite caution from her colleagues, this teacher was devoted to the development of successful African American students. Not only did she do that, but she also went on to educate other teachers who had problems with their Black students. In her opinion, education isn't a White/Black issue; it's a commitment issue. Teachers who have the same expectations for their White and Black students report similar results, especially if they're able to provide their Black students with some one-on-one attention. At the same time, teachers who have low expectations for their Black students report poor results. In this case, their attitude determined their approach and the results. It's important that you get to know your child's teacher and uncover her perceptions about achievement as early as you can, so you can make a switch if necessary.

Getting Passing Grades for Our Schools

Regardless of where you live, there are things that you can do to ensure that your child is well served by his school and educators. Try these suggestions:

- **Be assertive.** Determine whether your child's school has a comprehensive curriculum that is both educational and culturally sensitive, and then ensure that your child is enrolled in programs that allow him to take advantage of these benefits. Always push for challenging and advanced coursework for your child, even if he may only be able to take one or two courses initially.

- **Be active.** Let the other parents and teachers know that you're concerned about your child's education by joining the PTA, attending parent-teacher conferences, and voting in school board elections. Let your voice and vote count.
- **Be challenging.** If there is something that you don't like, let the teacher or principal know about it. Be respectful and constructive to ensure that your child doesn't suffer from unfair retaliation. In addition, make sure that you're talking to the right person about your concerns. The school principal is the appropriate person with whom to follow up your concerns regarding the teachers. The principal sets the tone for the building. If you find that the principal is not addressing your concerns, then contact the superintendent, who sets the tone for the school district.
- **Be organized.** Connect with other parents who share your concerns so you can share ideas, exchange information, and collectively discuss how you plan to make changes in the school.

You have the legal right to get your child the best education possible. Before you attempt to implement a host of changes, first determine what changes need to be made. Take an honest look at your school to see how it measures up to other schools that you know about.

School Assessment Tool

Are you ready to evaluate your child's school? Please review the following inventory guide to determine the facility's strengths and weaknesses. Once you have your results, start helping that school implement some necessary changes.

VO = Very Often
O = Often
S = Sometimes
NO = Not Often
N = Never

	VO	O	S	NO	N
Teachers communicate concerns to parent					
Teachers share positives and child's successes					
Administrators set the tone for diversity					
There is a plan for student progress					
Racial identity is acknowledged					
Teachers encourage students					
Parents are invited and welcomed					
Curriculum is culturally and racially inclusive					
Diversity is celebrated (e.g., Kwanzaa, Martin Luther King Day, Black History Month)					
Administrators interact with parents					

Chapter Eleven: The Role of the Community

Facilities such as recreational centers, Boys and Girls Clubs, and community-based organizations are needed now more than ever before. These amenities provide an alternative to "hanging out" while keeping children out of trouble. When we're talking about self-esteem, racial identity, and academic achievement, alternatives like these provide a boost in all of these areas.

Take my brother, Robert L. Powell Jr., for instance. He works with the youth in a Boys and Girls Club and his impact is phenomenal. He also works in a school where he designed a program that enables him to closely monitor the youth. Many of the children visit him a couple of times a day when he is in his office at the high school for support, direction, and to vent. My brother holds them accountable for their actions and encourages them to follow through on their goals and commitments. He keeps them on track. He makes sure they have their breakfast, complete their homework, and have properly reviewed their daily schedule. He also provides them with support throughout the day. For some, this is the only contact they have with a positive male role model and they see him as their parent away from home. This type of intervention is an excellent way of making sure that "at-risk" students graduate from high school.

Community leaders need to lobby for innovative and effective programs to reach our youth. These efforts, however, need to be outcome-driven, with measurable goals. Black American culture is built upon a foundation of strong community ties that can be traced back to our African origins. "I am because we are, and because we are, therefore, I am," wrote J.S. Mbiti in *African Religions and Philosophies*. In Africa, the dominant allegiance of our ancestors was to the tribe, a group that had many faces but also had a shared set of goals. Instead of focusing on the individual, they focused on the community. Collective survival, responsibility and a network of interconnected kinship helped

African people thrive. These lessons must also be applied to our communities today.

Afrocentricity, a concept that focuses on Black people celebrating the values, culture and history of Africa, is another benefit that African American children can enjoy by being involved in community-based activities and organizations. These organizations are not looking for validation from mainstream White culture but are based on fulfilling the unique needs of the communities they serve. Children who participate get to see other Blacks in leadership roles and are sometimes encouraged to contribute their own ideas to improve the current program. Thus, the objective of involving your children in Afrocentric community activities is twofold: 1) you want your children to enjoy a shared experience with other African Americans; and 2) you want your child to share his ideas in an environment where those suggestions will be used and valued.

Community Assessment Tool

How do you know if the community activity is a match for your child? Please review the following inventory guide to assess the programs in your community and your involvement. Once you have your results, start involving your child in activities that provide the best fit.

VO = Very Often
O = Often
S = Sometimes
NO = Not Often
N = Never

	VO	O	S	NO	N
Programs that celebrate Black history					
Celebrations such as Kwanzaa and Juneteenth					
Black arts such as theater, dance and drumming Rites of passage ceremonies for youth					
Literacy programs					
Black book clubs and support of African American literature					
Education focus in community events					
Respect and support to elders in the community					
Community projects and activism - voter registration					
Appreciation of other cultures and races					

Chapter Twelve: God Is in Charge!

I hope that you'll do everything you can to ensure that your child has academic success. As we come to a close, please remember that we are only stewards. Our children belong to God. They are gifts to us, for us to nurture and take care of, but we do not have full reign over them. I tell you that because there are only aspects of our lives and our children's experiences that we can control. The other parts are in God's hands; He has total control.

I am a Christian. However, regardless of your religion or denomination, most of us believe in a Higher Power and raise our children to have faith and values. Some of my friends are Jewish, Muslim, Baha'i, and other religions. The common thread is love of family and a desire to raise healthy children with positive self-esteem, identity and academic achievement. As you focus on your children's needs, be aware that they have spirits and souls that also need tender care. Know that what you say and do to them impacts their spiritual development. Your primary objective should be to bring them closer to God in all that you do.

Speaking as a Christian, as I honor and glorify Jesus Christ, my Savior, I encourage you to apply and adapt Christian principles to meet your family's needs. This is something that you're probably familiar with, since most African Americans grew up in the traditional Black church. Though I grew up Catholic, I still cherish the traditional Black church and have raised my children to worship there. I understand that historically, the Black church has been the foundation for many of our leaders and has served as a catalyst for change. It has been a place where African Americans could come together to determine ways to combat racism and oppression. The Black church has been an important tool in helping our people develop positive self-esteem and racial identity. In your quest to help your children excel, please don't leave that part of their development behind.

Prayer and faith have allowed the Black community to survive insurmountable odds and adversity. No matter the religion or denomination—Presbyterian; Methodist; Episcopalian; Baptist; Muslim; Pentecostal; Hindu; Buddhist; Jehovah's Witness; Jewish; Seventh-Day Adventist; or Yoruba, for instance—we all rely on a Higher Power for guidance. Some Blacks maintain a spiritual connection by reading inspirational books, meditating or studying various spiritual guides on their personal quests for inner knowledge. There are also spiritual Afrocentric traditions that include libations and honoring our ancestors. No matter what form with which you are most familiar, I want to remind you to keep God in the forefront. That connection will help you cope when nothing else can.

There are many unexpected things that can occur as we move through our lives. Illnesses, birth defects, or psychological issues are just a few of the complications that can pop up. As long as you rely on God, have faith, pray, and teach your children to do these things, you will be able to cope. It's no secret that African American families who turn to God for hope and inspiration, in good times and in bad, have a greater ability to overcome obstacles and meet challenges. Beyond that, understanding that God is in charge will enable you and your children to better deal with issues related to self-esteem, racial identity and academic achievement.

God's In Charge

VO = Very Often
O = Often
S = Sometimes
NO = Not Often
N = Never

	VO	O	S	NO	N
Pray alone					
Prays with family					
Worships					
Reads the Bible					
Demonstrates faith					
Recognizes the strength of the Black church					
Counts blessings and acknowledges good things					
Serves by helping others					
Gives to others when appropriate					
Believes in God's plan for your life					

APPENDIX

SENTENCE COMPLETION

Read these sentence stems to your child and have him respond. Older children may write the sentence completion themselves.

1. I like myself because . . .
2. I don't like myself because . . .
3. I look best when . . .
4. My hair is . . .
5. My nose is . . .
6. My skin color is . . .
7. School is . . .
8. People like me because . . .
9. People don't like me because . . .
10. My teacher thinks that I . . .
11. In school, I . . .
12. My friends say that I am . . .
13. My family loves me because . . .
14. My mom doesn't like me when I . . .
15. My mom likes me when I . . .
16. My dad likes when I . . .
17. My dad doesn't like when I . . .
18. Black people are . . .
19. White people are . . .
20. Black people should . . .
21. I am smart at . . .
22. I have trouble with . . .
23. If I were White, I would . . .
24. Someone treated me badly because I'm Black when . . .
25. My Black friends think that White people are . . .

This exercise allows you to gain awareness and insight into how your child thinks and feels about racial identity, self-esteem and academic achievement. Use it as a communication tool to discuss these issues with your child.

PARENT QUESTIONNAIRE

1. Black parents should teach their children that
   a) Everyone is treated equally
   b) The White man can't be trusted
   c) Black people are jealous of each other ("crabs in a barrel")
   d) There is good and bad in every race

2. When a Black child feels discriminated against, his parents should
   a) Tell him not to cry and be strong
   b) Confront the bigot
   c) Talk about why he felt mistreated
   d) Hold him and tell him how evil the world is

3. When a teacher gives a Black child a low grade, the parent should
   a) Make an appointment to talk to the teacher
   b) Tell the child to do better next time
   c) Call the principal
   d) Tell the child that with racist teachers, he has to be twice as good.

4. When a child makes a negative comment about her appearance and features, a parent should
   a) Tell her how ugly stringy-haired White girls are
   b) Take her to see Miss Black Teen
   c) Talk to her, listen, and tell her how beautiful she is
   d) Tell her that she can change her appearance when she gets older; *Extreme Makeover* is looking for candidates

5. When a baby is born, a parent should
   a) Describe the child's skin color and hair texture to relatives
   b) Act color blind and ignore the characteristics
   c) Tell people that the baby is loved and how it looks doesn't matter
   d) Tell people what you think is most attractive because the baby will change anyway

6. When a child starts preschool, it is important to
   a) Send the child with Black books and dolls/action figures
   b) See if the preschool has diverse materials
   c) Write a letter telling the administration about the importance of diversity
   d) Let your child play with White dolls and read White books in school and play with Black dolls and read Black books at home

7. What should a parent do to improve their child's expression of feelings about race?
   a) Stop the child from saying negative statements
   b) Correct the child and tell him something positive immediately
   c) Listen to the child, validate feelings, reassure and guide
   d) Encourage the child to be angry, it's a racist world

8. If someone uses a racial slur/racist remark toward your child, you should tell your child to
   a) Knock them upside the head
   b) Call the police

c) Confront them assertively and tell someone in authority
d) Ignore them, they are ignorant

9. What causes a child to have low self-esteem?
   a) Watching too much television
   b) Family members being negative and critical
   c) Going to a White friend's house
   d) Reading *Huckleberry Finn*

10. If your adolescent speaks Ebonics in front of your co-workers, you should
    a) Ask him to repeat himself
    b) Tell him you are going to knock the Black off of him
    c) Take him aside and tell him to speak standard English
    d) Ask him to play the piano, you need to show how cultured you are

Best answers:
1. D	6. B
2. C	7. C
3. A	8. C
4. C	9. B
5. A	10. C

These questions allow you to assess your judgment in dealing with parenting issues. Think about the text you've just read, especially as it relates to issues surrounding racial identity, self-esteem and academic achievement. The most appropriate answers were provided in the previous chapters.

Afrocentric Interventions for Psychologists, Social Workers, and Mental Health Professionals

In my clinical practice and at my consultation sites, I have designed and implemented a clinical model that focuses on Afrocentricity. It is based on the principles of Kwanzaa, the *Nguzo Saba*. The principles are universal and consistent with the Christian principles by which I live. The model addresses specific diagnostic criteria experienced by many of the children and families that come in for treatment. The primary diagnoses are:

- Anxiety disorder
- Depression and low self-esteem
- Post-traumatic stress disorder
- Oppositional defiant disorder
- Attention Deficit Hyperactivity Disorder

Anxiety symptoms include an unpleasant and unjustified sense of apprehension, often accompanied by physiological changes. Individuals may experience one or more of the following: tension, fear, irritability, heart palpitations, diarrhea, clammy hands, sweating, insomnia, fatigue and panic attacks.

The symptoms of depression, dysthymic disorder and low-self esteem include feelings of hopelessness and worthlessness; despair; low energy; fatigue; sleep disturbance; feelings of being immobilized; diminished emotional bonds; poor concentration; and interpersonal withdrawal.

On a continuum, low self-esteem is less severe than dysthymia, which can be characterized as low-level depressive feelings. Clinical depression is the most severe.

Post-traumatic stress disorder (PTSD) occurs when an individual suffers from a severe loss or stress such as a rape, car accident, natural disaster or war. The symptoms include anxiety; exaggerated or startled response; nightmares; intrusive thoughts; reliving the feelings experienced at the time of the trauma; and avoidance of anything associated with the trauma.

Oppositional defiant disorder (ODD) is when an individual defies authority; is oppositional; disobedient; confrontational; defiant; disruptive; and has difficulty following rules.

Attention deficit hyperactivity disorder (ADHD) is when an individual is highly distractible; inattentive; impulsive; quick tempered; restless; and has a low tolerance for frustration.

Therapists should be warm, empathic, understanding and optimistic when working with clients. Clinical interventions should be innovative and culturally relevant.

These interventions are geared toward fostering family bonding, connectedness and communication. Afrocentric interactive approaches include family activities such as:
- Drumming
- Afrocentric crafts, like mask making
- Creative writing and sharing
- Reading and discussion of African American literature, Black history and spiritual/inspirational books.

Drumming is focused on using the *djembe* drum as a clinical intervention. The beat, tempo and instruction vary depending on the diagnosis. For example, individuals with depressive disorders are inspired to play a more upbeat, fast tempo while individuals with anxiety disorders are inspired to play slower, more relaxing beats. Positive self-talk is developed in order to address the particular problem. For example, a person diagnosed with depression will recite or chant, "I feel uplifted, energized and joyful." Children and adolescents with ODD or ADHD will focus on controlling their impulses, concentrating, and following directions. Individuals with adjustment disorders and PTSD will focus on positive self-talk related to dealing with stressors, life changes or trauma. Drumming will reflect their need to express feelings related to their experiences and work it through.

Afrocentric crafts, which include mask making, focus on creativity and use of the finished product as a tool for self-expression. The family members share their creations with each other and openly discuss feelings, experiences, hopes and dreams.

Writing and reading focuses on literacy and bibliotherapy as a means of gaining insight and understanding. It is also a way to inspire sharing, closeness, and communication. Family members are encouraged to journal, read relevant African American literature, Black history and spiritual material. This is used in sessions as a way of exploring unresolved issues, unexpressed emotions and experiences. Family members are also encouraged to share their poems, stories, letters or journal entries. This disclosure and open communication is used to foster greater family bonding, connectedness and understanding.

In-Home Interventions
- Soulful cooking
- Environmental makeovers; cleaning, decoration and decluttering
- Pampering (facials, pedicures, manicures, massages)
- African/cultural dance
- Family projects (family photo albums, memory books)

Clinical Diagnosis and Goals

Below are the goals and behavioral outcomes for the aforementioned clinical disorders. These goals and behavioral changes are a direct result of implementing Afrocentric interventions in your child's life.

Diagnosis: Depression and/or low self-esteem

Goal: To increase feelings of faith, joy and confidence while decreasing feelings of hopelessness frustration and sadness.

Behavioral outcome:
- Increased involvement in positive, pro-social activities
- Increase in positive self-statements
- Self-report of increased feelings of faith and joy
- Decrease in negative self-statements

Diagnosis: Anxiety

Goal: To increase feelings of security and confidence and decrease feelings of anxiety and insecurity.

Behavioral outcome: Increased involvement in positive activities that were previously prohibited due to anxiety

Diagnosis: Post-traumatic stress disorder (PTSD) or adjustment disorders

Goal: To increase feelings of safety and security while decreasing feelings of anxiety related to trauma or life adjustment and intrusive thoughts

Behavioral outcome: Increased involvement in desired activities related to the history of stress or trauma, without interference of negative emotional or physiological symptoms

Diagnosis: Oppositional Defiant Disorder (ODD)

Goal: To increase compliance and cooperation and decrease oppositional, defiant behavior

Behavioral outcome: Increased responsiveness to following directions and adhering to rules

Diagnosis: Attention Deficit Hyperactivity Disorder (ADHD)

Goal: To increase attention and concentration

Behavioral outcome: Increased focus and time on tasks

Outcome measures are pre- and post-structured interviews. They can occur with the individual via a self-report, or with family members. Key information is gathered from these sources as well as the primary clinicians' report, school report, community resources and church, when available. The self-report focuses on a decrease in symptoms related to the diagnosis.

Therapists and/or group leaders should identify precipitants to behaviors related to the diagnosis. What happens in the immediate moments prior to the acting out or defiant behavior of a child? It is important to identify exactly what the behavior is. For example, a depressed woman may isolate herself. In this case, the consequences of the behavior should be identified. A man experiencing PTSD may end up getting arrested after he assaulted someone, during an episode where he had an intrusive recollection of a traumatic event. For ODD and ADHD, clear contingencies need to be established with consequences and rewards, in order to shape pro-social behaviors.

The goal should be to move from extrinsic rewards, such as material objects, to fostering intrinsic rewards like praise, which leads to feeling good. Alternative behaviors should be identified for the individual. For example, instead of acting out when a child is provoked in school, he will count to ten and visualize playing a specific beat on the drum that is calming. A child who is easily distracted may concentrate on a particular object in a room while thinking of affirmations that help him focus. Behaviors and approaches that help in the session should be transferable to home and school. There should be a gradual increase of time on task to improve focus, concentration, compliance and cooperation.

Using the seven principles of Kwanzaa, therapists or group leaders should have the family assess themselves and ultimately develop affirmations focused on cognitive restructuring to change negative self or family statements into positive, affirming ones. Family members should be able to identify and connect with each principle.

Nguzo Saba

The assessment questions can be modified for younger children to make them developmentally appropriate. Answer them using the Likert scale answers (Very True, Somewhat True, Not True at All)

Umoja (Unity): *To strive for and maintain unity in the family, community, nation, and race.*
- Identify underlying causes of the feelings and symptoms
- Identify family activities that are interactive
- Identify common family goals or mission statement
- Establish goals related to interactive family activities

Assessment

VT = Very True
ST = Somewhat True
NT = Not True At All

	VT	ST	NT
My family gets along well			
My family spends time together			
My family is united			
My family works out problems well			
My family supports each other			

Our family is _____

_____

Our family shows support by _____

_____

Our family shows love by _____

_____

When our family has a problem, we _____

_____

Our family doesn't _____

_____

Affirmations

I feel joy in having unity with my family.

I am connected to my family and enjoy interacting with them.

Ujima (Collective Work and Responsibility): *To build and maintain our community together and make our brother's and sister's problems our problems and to solve them together.*

- Identify support networks
- Identify community activities in which the family engages
- Identify extended family relationships
- Identify degree of positive support
- Identify projects and collective work that the family is involved in
- Identify members of family who may be estranged, ostracized or distants

Assessment

VT = Very True
ST = Somewhat True
NT = Not True At All

	VT	ST	NT
My family works well together			
My family spends time together			
My family helps one another			
My family is responsible			
My family solves problems together			
My family reaches out to others			

Our family works together when _____

_____

I wish my family would help me more when _____

_____

The members of my family who I would like to be more responsible are _____

_____

I would like a member of my family to be more responsible because _____

_____

In my family, collective work means _____

_____

Affirmations

    I work well with my family

    I can be responsible in working with others

    We can do it together

***Kujichaguilia* (Self-Determination):** *To define ourselves, name ourselves, create for ourselves and speak for ourselves.*
- Identify religious or spiritual beliefs
- Define self-esteem
- Define racial identity
- Define individual, family goals and mission statement
- Identify self-esteem challenges
- Identify racial identity issues
- Identify self statements/cognitions related to self-esteem and self-efficacy

Assessment

VT = Very True
ST = Somewhat True
NT = Not True At All

	VT	ST	NT
My family is motivated			
My family is strong			
My family has power to change our circumstance			
My family makes good decisions			
My family follows through with commitments			

Our family is determined to _____

Our family is powerful because _____
_____

Our family speaks up when _____
_____

Our family decides how to _____
_____

Our family is empowered by _____
_____

Racism hurts my family because _____
_____

My family can't get ahead because _____
_____

People hurt my family by _____
_____

People try to oppress my family by _____
_____

My family has trouble dealing with _____
_____

Affirmations
    My family and I know who we are and our purpose in life
    We can do what we commit to

Ujamma (Cooperative Economics): *To build and maintain our own stores, shops, and other businesses and to profit from them together.*
- Identify financial resources
- Identify cooperative approaches to finances
- Assess financial stress
- Explore lifestyle choices
- Assess degree of materialism vs. financial ability

Assessment

VT = Very True
ST = Somewhat True
NT = Not True At All

	VT	ST	NT
My family finances are good			
My family does not spend in excess			
My family does not live beyond our means			
My family shares resources			
My family has everything we need			

Our family budgets by _____
_____

Our family supports one another by _____
_____

When there are financial difficulties in my family, we _____
_____

My family's financial planning includes _____
_____

My family owns _____
_____

Affirmations

- I will live financially within my means
- My family will be prosperous
- My family members help each other

***Nia* (Purpose):** *To make our collective vocation the building and developing of our community in order to restore our people to their traditional greatness.*
- Identify family goals
- Identify community involvement
- Assess individual goals and aspirations
- Develop or revisit family mission statement
- Assess level of motivation

Assessment

VT = Very True
ST = Somewhat True
NT = Not True At All

	VT	ST	NT
My family knows our purpose in life			
My family does great things			
My family gives to each other			
My family works together			
My family is highly motivated			

Our family's purpose is _____

_____

When my family works together, we _____

_____

Our family is motivated to _____

_____

Our family goals are _____

_____

Our family supports each other's goals by _____

_____

Affirmations

- My family has a purpose
- My family is restoring our people to greatness
- My family is building our community

***Kummba* (creativity):** *To do always as much as we can, in the way we can, in order to leave our community more beautiful and beneficial than we inherited it.*
- Identify healthy family outlets
- Identify creative family outlets
- Identify positive family memories and experiences
- Assess what legacy the family would like to leave
- Assess levels of creative thinking and innovative ideas

Assessment

VT = Very True
ST = Somewhat True
NT = Not True At All

	VT	ST	NT
My family gives to the community			
My family is involved in creating family experiences			
My family expresses ourselves in unique ways			
My family values the beauty of nature			
My family respects creative things			

Our family shows creativity by _____

_____

In our family, beauty is seen in _____

_____

Our family adds to our community by _____

_____

Our community benefits from my family because _____

_____

Creativity is respected in my family because _____

_____

Affirmations

    I am creative in giving to my family and community

    I am committed to supporting my family and community

***Imani* (faith):** *To believe with all our heart, in our people, our parents, our teachers, our leaders and the righteousness and victory of our struggle.*

- Assess connection to people from the African Diaspora
- Assess belief in honoring ancestors
- Assess relationship and trust in our teachers
- Assess commitment to the struggle of African American people

Assessment

VT = Very True
ST = Somewhat True
NT = Not True At All

	VT	ST	NT
My family is connected to the African Diaspora			
My family has faith in African American people			
My family has faith in our teachers			
My family has faith in our leaders			
My family has a commitment to the struggle of African American people			

Our family shows faith by _____

_____

Faith in our family means _____

_____

We show faith in our teachers by _____

_____

We show faith in our leaders by _____

_____

Our struggle as a people involves _____

_____

Affirmations

    My family has great faith

    Our community is strong and victorious

    My family believes that all things work for good for those who love the Lord

Resources

Education

In The Black: The African American Parent's Guide to Raising Financially Responsible Children by Fran Harris (Fireside, 1998)

The Black-White Test Score Gap by Christopher Jencks and Meredith Phillips (Brookings Institute Press, 1998)

For Parents

Achievement Matters: Getting Your Child the Best Education Possible by Hugh B. Price (Dafina Books, 2003)

Dr. Spock's Baby and Child Care: A Handbook for Parents of Developing Children from Birth through Adolescence by Benjamin Spock, MD (Dutton Books, 1998)

Gifted Hands by Ben Carson, MD (Zondervan Publishing Company, 1996)

Saving Our Sons: Raising Black Children in a Turbulent World by Marita Golden (Doubleday, 1994)

The Joy and Challenge of Raising African American Children by Emma M. Talbott

The Skin We're In: Teaching Our Children to Be Emotionally Strong, Socially Smart, and Spiritually Connected by Janie Victoria Ward (Free Press, 2000)

Waiting for a Miracle by Dr. James Comer (E.P. Dutton, 1997)

Why Are All the Black Kids Sitting Together in the Cafeteria? And Other Conversations About Race by Beverly Daniel Tatum, Ph.D. (Basic Books, 2003)

Recreational

African American Folktales for Young Readers by Richard Alan Young and Judy Dockrey Young (August House Publishes, 1997)

How the Spider Became Bald: Folktales and Legends from West Africa by Peter Eric Adotey Addo (Morgan Reynolds Publishers, 1993)

ABOUT THE AUTHOR

Darlene Powell-Garlington, Ph.D. is a practicing clinical psychologist who specializes in individual and family therapy, evaluations and consultations. She is also a certified school psychologist.

In 1990, Dr. Powell-Garlington received the NAACP's Distinguished Service Award. Her research on children's racial attitudes and doll color preferences received national recognition in over 300 newspapers and magazines including *The New York Times, Chicago Tribune, Los Angeles Times, Washington Post, USA Today, Time, Newsweek, Ebony, Parenting, Child,* and *Cosmopolitan*.

Since then she has maintained a private practice in psychology and has worked as a consultant to schools, organizations and corporations such as the Nickelodeon Television Network and Mattel Inc., on issues relating to Black children. Throughout the year she conducts workshops, speaking engagements, and retreats all over the U.S., focusing on her areas of expertise and published books. Most frequently, the issues discussed are diversity, interpersonal communication, women's concerns, self-esteem of African American children, parenting and family dynamics.

Dr. Powell-Garlington is coauthor of six books: *Different and Wonderful: Raising Black Children in a Race-Conscious Society* (Simon and Schuster, 1990), *Raising the Rainbow Generation* (Fireside, 1993); *Teaching Your Children To Be Successful in a Multicultural Society* (Fireside, 1993), *Friend, Lovers and Soul Mates: A Guide to Better Relationships Between Black Men and Women* (Simon & Schuster, 1995), *Juba This and Juba That: 100 African American Games for Children* (Fireside, 1996), *The Power of Soul: Pathways to*

Psychological and Spiritual Growth for African Americans (William Morrow, 1997), and *Team-Spirited Parenting: Eight Essential Principles for Parenting Success* (John Wiley & Sons, 2001).

Because of her reputation as an author and consultant, and having received significant media exposure in her career, Dr. Powell-Garlington has been and is a frequent guest on dozens of radio shows and some well-known television programs and stations, including *Good Morning America*, *20/20*, ABC News, Black Entertainment Television, *Geraldo*, *Ricki Lake*, *Montel*, *Tony Brown's Journal*, *The McCreary Report*, *America's Black Forum*, and numerous others. She was a consultant and frequent guest on *The John Walsh Show*. Dr. Powell-Garlington also contributes monthly advice columns to *Today's Black Woman* and *Black Entertainment Television* magazines and has been a psychological consultant for Disney Online's *Family.com*

Dr. Powell-Garlington is also the founder and CEO of Legacy Consultation Services, a national tutoring service that matches children and families with tutors. Legacy Consultation Services provides psychological and educational consultation services for children and families. The philosophy of LEGACY is to build positive self-esteem and racial identity in children, which inspires and motivates them to do well academically. ED-U-CARE is the branch of LEGACY, which provides tutoring services for Black children. Educators who genuinely care provide the solution to academic achievement challenges with Black children. ED-U-CARE is comprehensive and culturally relevant because it incorporates proven educational techniques with innovative approaches, which makes learning fun and interesting.

Dr. Powell-Garlington lives with her two children, Dotti, age 17, and Derek, age 12; and her husband, Dr. Ernest C. Garlington, in Marion, Connecticut.